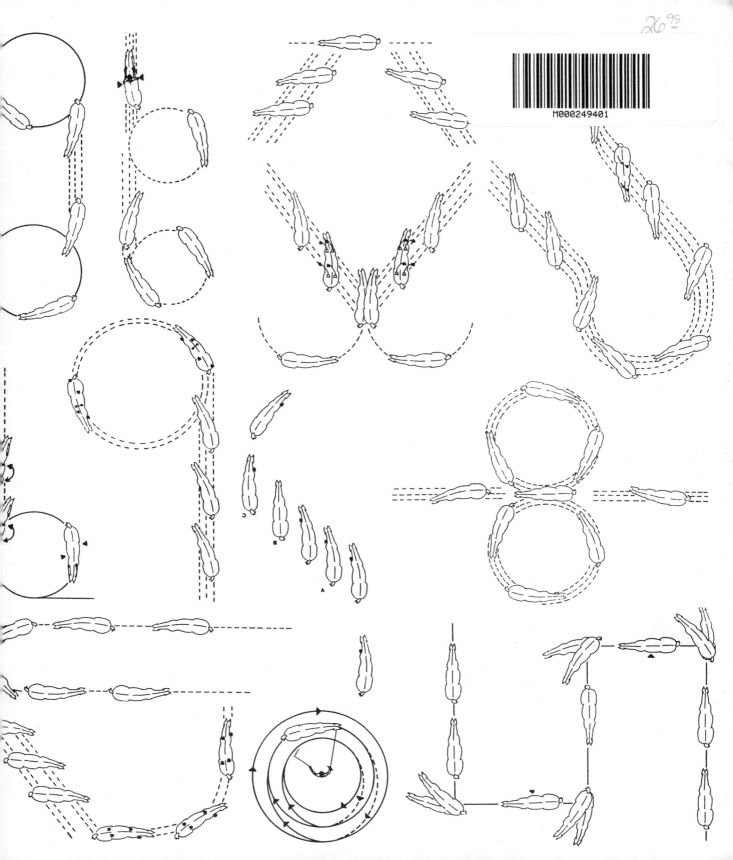

COMMON SENSE
DRESSAGE

Lynda —
you always
had it — you'll
be a 1st class
rider & Mcourage
you to use your
talent! So much love
your real mom —
xoxox

COMMON SENSE DRESSAGE

An Illustrated Guide

by Sally O'Connor

With a Foreword by Robert Dover

Illustrations by Jean L. Schucker

Half Halt Press
Middletown, Maryland

COMMON SENSE DRESSAGE:
An Illustrated Guide
© 1990 Sally Ann O'Connor

Published 1990 in the United States of America by
Half Halt Press, Inc.
6416 Burkittsville Road
Middletown, MD 21769

Illustrations © Jean L. Schucker
Photos © George E. Perentesis, except as otherwise noted.
Excerpts from the *Rules of Dressage* printed with the kind permission
of the Federation Equestre Internationale.

Book and jacket design by Clara Graves
Cover Photo by Tim Davis
Printed in the United States of America

Library of Congress Cataloging-in-Publication Data

O'Connor, Sally.
    Common sense dressage : an illustrated guide / by Sally O'Connor :
with a foreword by Robert Dover : illustrations by Jean L. Schucker.
       p.   cm.
     Includes index.
     ISBN 0-939481-21-9
      1. Dressage.   2. Dressage horses--Training.   I. Title.
SF309.5.026 1990
798.2'3--dc20
                                                    90-5375
                                                    CIP

This book is dedicated with great respect
to the memory of

NUNO OLIVEIRA

TABLE OF CONTENTS

FOREWORD

Sally O'Connor has devoted her entire life to the equestrian world with particular emphasis on the art of dressage. In her travels she has seen how difficult it can be for people living in outlying areas to receive quality instruction.

I was, therefore, delighted when she told me of her new book, **Common Sense Dressage**, and was even more excited after having read the manuscript. Sally's approach to training the dressage horse details many refreshingly practical techniques and her wide use of diagrams and photographs help to clarify for the less experienced trainer the more subtle problems and objectives of dressage.

Common Sense Dressage will prove to be an invaluable aid to riders and trainers all over and especially those who find it impossible to stay under constant supervision of a professional.

ACKNOWLEDGMENTS

This book owes its existence to a great many people who have contributed their expertise and time with generosity.

The training techniques outlined I learned from some great teachers beginning with Betty Howett and Lockie Richards and progressing on to Franz Rockowansky of the Spanish Riding School who converted me from a basic dressage necessary for eventing to an understanding of the classical precepts of advanced dressage; Colonel Bengt Ljungquist who patiently developed an eye for the "truth" in performance and above all to Nuno Oliveira who demonstrated a whole new dimension in lightness, balance and pure horsemanship.

The book itself was made possible by the patience and good humor of the photographers, especially George Parentesis who spent hours obtaining just the right pictures. The line drawings contributed by Jean Schucker make the exercises clear for all to understand—not an easy task.

Gene Freeze and Felicitas von Neumann-Cosel of First Choice Farm have been unfailing in their support and gave freely of their advice and time beyond any expectations and deserve lasting gratitude—one of the joys of the horse world is the friendships made over the years.

Thanks also to Beth Carnes of Half Halt Press for her cheerful and competent help and her belief in the book during the long process of assembling all the parts, at times an interminable task.

INTRODUCTION

Riding horses and training horses are two separate challenges. To train a horse you need to have a clear idea of what a horse is, how it moves, how it reacts to outside stimuli, and you must understand how a horse learns. Books on training exist in the thousands, outlining various methods, and the majority seem to indicate that if you do this, and then this, presto—you will have a trained horse. Not so—the making of a well trained horse is a long, difficult, and frustrating road, full of potholes and breakdowns. Each horse is an individual and what works with one won't necessarily work with the next—it depends on the horse. While training should be guided by classical principles, the way you arrive at a result can vary from horse to horse.

Persistence and knowledge are the keys to successful training. Good help or instruction are not readily available in all parts of the world; often you have to go it alone and learn by trial and error. The aim of this book is to set out a sequential system of training, pointing out some of the major pitfalls and offering suggestings on solving problems that can and will arise during the program.

Not everyone has the perfect horse, the Grand Prix dressage prospect; the vast majority of us have to work with what we have. I do not think that the perfect horse exists. A horse is a horse: there are small horses, tall horses, long horses and short horses, thin horses and fat horses, slow horses and fast horses, phlegmatic horses and hysterical horses. You have to train according to type. There is no such animal as a "dressage horse"—there are horses and all can be trained. Dressage can and will improve any horse no matter what its ultimate use in life may be.

The horse evolved slowly over the ages from a furtive little creature with three toes that lived in the marshes to a larger one-toed animal that grazed on wide grassy plains and roamed in herds for protection. Scientists believe that horses were probably domesticated around 3,000 B.C., after the dog and cattle.

The horse had many natural predators, many of which jumped on its back to bring it down and kill it. Flight was its main defense and, accordingly, the horse developed keen eyesight and an acute perception of any outside movement.

The social structure of the herd developed for the protection of the species. The dominant lead mare ran the show, with the rest following her lead. Herd conditioning makes the horse an apt pupil, as trainer you can replace the chain of command and use the horse's natural instinct to obey in your favor. Domination does not preclude cooperation however; your horse can be conditioned to be a willing partner rather than a subservient slave if you go about training in the correct manner.

The backyard horse who lives alone is deprived of the companionship of other horses and you must replace some of that need. Horses that are kept in "prison like" stables where they cannot see other horses around them can develop neurotic behavior. An open-type plan in a stable where the horse feels it is living in a herd situation is highly preferable to a closed-in stall life. Iron bars and high walls may be attractive to the human eye but are unnatural for the sociable horse — nervousness, cribbing, weaving, stall walking are all man-made neuroses.

To train a horse you must learn to react like a horse and realize that what may seem like willful behavior at times is merely the horse's way of letting you

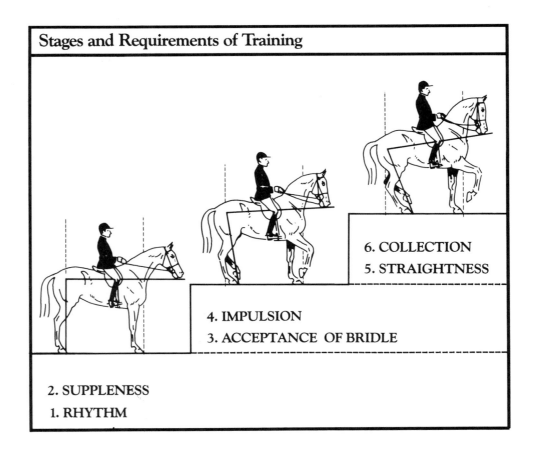

Stages and Requirements of Training

6. COLLECTION
5. STRAIGHTNESS
4. IMPULSION
3. ACCEPTANCE OF BRIDLE
2. SUPPLENESS
1. RHYTHM

know it does not understand what you want. Above all you must remember that horses do not think and reason as we do; they are highly instinctive. Horses are capable of attachments but do not have human emotions; they can attach themselves to the trainer, but they just as readily attach themselves to whoever shows up with the feed bucket. They form attachments among themselves if stabled or pastured together, but form new attachments if one leaves. While your horse will not pine if you go away for a week, it will not forget you and your actions. You must do everything in your power to win your horse's trust so that it will have the confidence it needs to be able to learn. A frightened or agitated horse is in no condition to learn. Like kids, the more horses learn the more they are capable of learning. You build their minds and bodies skill by skill as you introduce new exercises. You do not teach calculus to a small child, you first must teach it one plus one. Likewise, you do not go out and teach your horse flying changes every stride in the first lesson; you begin by teaching it to balance itself in canter and work from there.

The basics are the foundation. If you take great pains in the beginning stages of training, you will find the more advanced work comes easily because the horse has been prepared mentally and physically, and is willing to attempt new lessons, having understood the learning process. When you teach a new skill you must learn to recognize even the slightest indication of a correct response and reinforce the lesson by stopping and caressing the horse. "Lots of pats" is a phrase I use often. Patting not only gives the horse a pleasant feeling, it also serves to relax its muscles.

Horses are tactile animals, "touchy-feelie," and you can use this to advantage in training. In the herd, horses indulge in mutual grooming; when we groom our

Six year old Irish TB mare. Well balanced with great strength in the short back and a powerful rear end. An elastic mover with a lot of suspension but a bit difficult to bend because of her short body, and her short, thick neck. She is super sensitive but willing.

Six year old TB/connemara gelding. A complete contrast with the previous photo: a long weak back with a straight and weak hindquarter. He has great difficulty in balance and engagement, with little or no suspension, and is locked in the front. This horse had been started in draw reins and was totally locked in shoulder and neck—a difficult horse to train.

horses we are using a natural behavior pattern for our own purpose. A horse can feel a fly on its side, so it stands to reason that it has to be able to feel you on its back—as long as you do not make it "tune you out."

Although not everyone will be starting with an unbroken horse, raw material to be molded into a well trained responsive animal (the ideal way to go), the methods for beginning training can be applied to any animal, and can be used with good results on spoiled or difficult horses that need rehabilitation. Many of the horses I have worked with came to me because they were "dangerous" or "impossible" but I find there are few "bad" horses, just horses that have been mistreated and badly started. Once they are given a chance most difficult horses prove to be quite trainable.

Ten year old quarter horse gelding. A little horse with a great deal of power behind. He has super natural suspension, but needed to become lighter and less restricted in front. A willing worker and surprisingly elastic when lateral work was introduced. He events at the Intermediate level.

Twelve year old TB gelding. A horse you might not look at seriously standing in the stall, with his long back and straight hind end. But he has tremendous natural suspension, a strong back, and great elasticity in spite of his shape!

Four year old trakhener/quarter horse gelding. A real challenge: not only is he much too long, his neck is on upside down and his temperament is unwilling. With careful training, he has developed into a light and balanced Fourth level horse—but it took a great deal of patience and faith during the first two years of training.

Age, of course, does make a difference; a horse learns the most between the ages of 4 to 8. After that, they are more set in their ways, and the older they are the less you will be able to re-educate their minds and muscles. The 16 year old that runs off will still run off. There are no miracles guaranteed, but sometimes you can work what seem to be miracles with patience and skill.

A word of warning: you will make mistakes. I have made hundreds and still do, but hopefully you should learn from each. Each horse you work with becomes easier to deal with as you increase your knowledge. A basic computer program is just that—basic—but you can keep adding to it until you have a highly sophisticated program with a great many options to call on. Training is like that, you keep adding options as you study and ride, and you then have a large memory bank to draw upon when confronted with a problem. I've been fortunate to work with some great trainers who shared freely from their memory banks. I find that good trainers have no secrets but share freely of their wisdom; I would like to pass some of that knowledge along.

◇1◇
THE HORSE: HOW IT FUNCTIONS

"A horse is a horse is a horse of course" went the old TV jingle—but just *what* is a horse?

A horse is a large quadruped with a highly developed set of instincts, acute eyesight and socially inclined. It reacts instinctively to outside movement, objects, sounds and smells, and flight is its main defense. All this must be borne in mind when you train a horse. A horse does not reason things out as we do, it reacts. A good trainer uses this to advantage; if you understand how a horse will react to something, you can make it react the way you want it to and build up sets of conditioned reflexes.

Getting down to bare bones, when you look at the horse's skeletal structure it is quickly apparent that the horse's spine supports its entire weight. None of the horse's weight lies on top of its spine but is suspended and supported from the spine. The horse's back, therefore, is a key factor in how it manages its locomotion. In riding, we come along and park ourselves right on top of the spine, a structure that was not designed to carry any weight—a fact that needs to be uppermost in our mind.

The head is a large mass of bone supported by a flexible neck. A horse's balance depends upon how it uses the head and neck to offset the greater mass of the

The flexible neck.

body. The neck allows the horse to drop its head and graze, and bends easily from side to side (watch a horse scratch its muzzle with a hind hoof or snap at a fly on its side). The neck vertebrae run down into the withers and continue along the back. However, there is no bone that connects the spine to the shoulder blades or the front legs—the horse has no collarbone.

The shoulder blades are cradled in a great mass of muscles and tissue above the forelegs. The spine from the withers back is supported by eighteen pairs of ribs: the first eight pairs connected by the breastbone, the next nine connected by cartilage and the final pair shorter and unattached, known as the "floating rib."

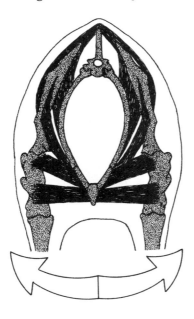

The shoulder blades are cradled in a great mass of muscles and tissue. There is no direct bony connection with the spine, thus allowing for a lateral displacement of the forelegs.

Behind the eighteen thoracic vertebrae lie six lumbar vertebrae (in some Arabian horses only five, in this case there is an extra thoracic bone). These lumbar vertebrae form the loin and play an important role in the manner in which the horse moves. Behind these lies the sacrum made up of five solidly fused vertebrae. At the end of the spine are eighteen tail bones.

In contrast to the flexible neck vertebrae, the thoracic vertebrae are rigid; this is where we place the saddle and our weight, as close to the strongest part of the spine as possible. The loin and lumbar vertebrae have some flexibility, but not a great deal. Unlike the dog and the cat which can arch their backs upwards, the horse can only arch its spine to a limited degree, but that arching is all important to the engagement of the hindlegs.

The hind leg of the horse is attached to the spine at the pelvic bone in the lumbosacral joint, perhaps the key joint in the body as it serves to transmit the thrust created by the hindleg to the spine and the entire body.

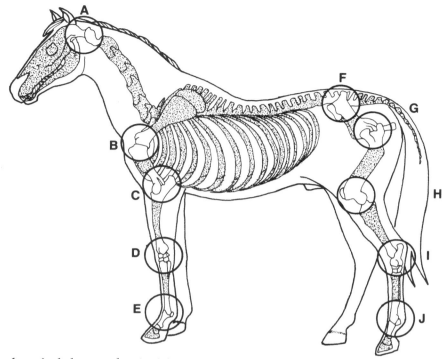

The horse's skeleton and major joints.
A. Poll, *where head is joined to neck and spine* **B.** *Shoulder joint* **C.** *Elbow* **D.** *Knee* **E.** *Fetlock*
F. *Pelvis and lumbosacral joint* **G.** *Hip joint* **H.** *Stifle joint* **I.** *Hock* **J.** *Fetlock*

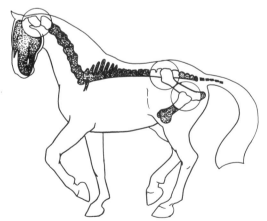

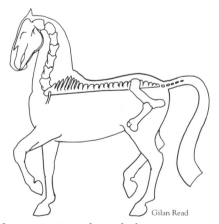

Gilan Read

Dressage training's ultimate goal is to engage the hindquarter and raise the forehand so it becomes flexible and light. The topline should become stretched giving true elevation of the forehand and a lowering of the hindquarter due to increased bending of the joints of the hindlegs.

Incorrect training forces the horse into a preconceived "frame" with a rigid spine and no real engagement behind. The horse "snatches" its legs up but is not truly engaged and becomes stiff and rigid in its movement and ultimately sore and/or lame in the spine or hindlegs.

The bones and joints of the hindleg are:

    a. the pelvic bone and the lumbosacral joint

    b. the femur, or thigh bone reaching from the hip joint to the stifle joint

    c. the tibia and fibula lying between the stifle and hock joints

    d. the tarsus or hock joint made up of six small bones

    e. the metatarsal bones, or cannon bone and splint bones

    f. the phalanges, long pastern, short pastern, and pedal or coffin bone

The bones and joints of the foreleg have no direct bony connection to the spine. One advantage of this is that the muscles and ligaments that support the foreleg absorb much of the concussion created by the forefeet striking the ground, thus protecting the spine. From top to bottom the bones and joints of the foreleg are:

    a. the scapula, or shoulder blade, forming the shoulder joint with

    b. the humerus or armbone, reaching from the point of the shoulder to the elbow

    c. the radius and ulna, two bones fused together reaching from the elbow to the knee

    d. the carpus or knee joint, made up of seven small bones

    e. the metacarpal bones, the cannon bone and split bones

    f. the fetlock joint joining the cannon bone and the first phalanx or long pastern

    g. the second phalanx or short pastern

    h. the third phalanx or pedal bone

So we see that "the head bone's connected to the neck bone, the neck bone's connected to the back bone. . . ." and "dem bones, dem bones gonna walk around." All these "dry bones" are held together and function through the means of a highly sophisticated system of checks and pulleys known as muscles, ligaments and tendons, all of which act and react upon each other, every action having a reaction. The muscles are the means by which the horse moves the skeleton, the ligaments and tendons attach muscles to the bones so they can be moved.

Dressage training is a system by which the trainer uses a logical progression of exercises to build and strengthen the muscular system to enable the horse to become a gymnast.

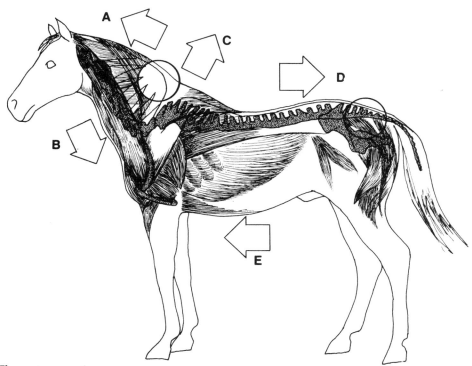

The major muscle groups.
A. *The muscles of the upper neck serve to raise the head and allow the forearm to move freely.*
B. *The muscles of the lower neck work in conjunction with those above to flex and bend the neck and extend the forearm.* **C.** *The muscles of the shoulder allow for extension and the spring necessary for collection and passage.* **D.** *The all-important muscles of the top of the spine allow the horse to carry the rider and connect the back limbs with the forehand.* **E.** *The muscles of the abdomen help the horse engage the hind legs under the body.*

These groups of muscles all work in opposition to each other: when you stretch one group, the opposite group contracts. Flexibility is developed as the muscles stretch and contract with elasticity. A "stiff" horse is one with contracted muscles that cannot stretch on one side or another.

The bones and muscles are covered by flesh and skin containing thousands of nerves and nerve endings that transmit sensation to the brain, transmissions that are then transformed into action. The brain is akin to a major telephone exchange handling incoming and outgoing messages. Your job as a trainer is to send the correct message to produce the desired answer. Messages are carried from nerve branches emanating from the spinal chord.

The spinal chord runs directly from the brain down the entire spine. It lies in a special channel of bony arches on top of each vertebrae for protection. The chord ends in the middle of the sacrum.

The spine then serves *not only as the support of the entire body*, but also *serves as a channel for the entire nervous system*. When you are sitting on the horse's back, you are sitting on the most important weight bearing structure and message center. The trick to getting results is to learn to *communicate with the horse's back*, because this communication is *completely natural* to the horse—a fact not always stressed in books on equitation.

When you first learn to ride your instructor teaches you rudimentary aids, like "Kick to make him go" or "Pull the reins to stop him or turn." The struggle to maintain your balance in the saddle takes much of your concentration. As important to understanding how the horse is put together is the need to understand how your own body works. Our skeleton is quite different, we have two legs and stand upright.

If the lumbosacral joint is the most important joint in the horse's body, I would like to say that the hip joint is the most important joint in the rider's body.

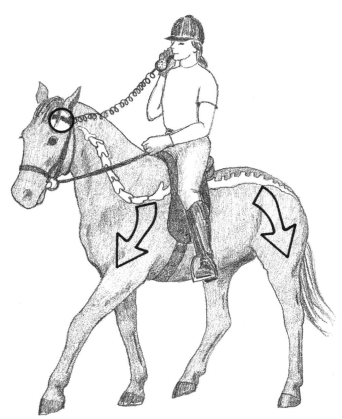

Messages are delivered via the nervous system to activate the muscles and limbs.

In order to balance the human spine, the hip joint must be flexible enough to absorb the movement of the horse and to move in harmony with it. The position of the rider's body in the saddle and in relation to the horse's spine makes the difference between being able to sit on a horse and being able to be an accomplished trainer. A trainer must have an understanding of both skeletons; the two must move in balance and harmony. There is nothing static about riding a horse: if you sit on something that moves, you must move with it. Being in total control of your body is a prerequisite if you are to control the horse's body—understanding how the horse moves helps achieve this control.

The success of giving an aid depends not upon the strength with which it is given but the exactness of the timing. If a horse is in the correct position, its legs in the proper place, the aid will transmit the correct message and it will be easy for the horse to obey. An aid given at the wrong moment can confuse the horse, confusion leads to resistance, and training goes backwards not forwards. An understanding of the timing of the aids depends on knowing exactly how the horse places its feet at each step. This knowledge makes life much simpler for both horse and rider, and leads to "equestrian tact."

A horse cannon read your mind, but it can and does read your body. Always remember that to give an aid: you must first think of it in your brain, your brain transmits the message to your body, the aid is given, and is felt by the horse's body. The message then goes to the horse's brain and is sent back to its body to produce the required response. There are six steps between the idea and the resulting action.

Horses go as we ride them.

◇2◇
LUNGEING

Lungeing for the horse

Lungeing is indispensable in training the young horse and can also be effective in retraining a horse that needs to be balanced and suppled. Eventually the horse must be able to carry the rider and perform, but lungeing allows the horse to develop its own muscles and balance without the burden of the rider's weight on its back.

Once the horse has learned the basic requirements of lunge work, when it knows it must go forward promptly on a circle at a required gait, you can teach many beneficial exercises while still on the lunge.

Over the years I have been exposed to many different theories and methods of lungeing, and the method I use now has brought me the most success with many different types of horses, from the unbroken horse to the crooked, stiff, unbalanced horse. The exercises vary but the technique remains constant.

A lungeing cavesson with a fixed nosepiece is an investment that will last a lifetime and is vital for successful lungeing. It is possible to lunge from the bridle, but you are then interfering with the action of the bit in the horse's mouth and can create more problems than you will solve. A lungeing cavesson makes it possible to work the horse without putting uneven pressure on the mouth.

The second piece of equipment needed is a lungeing surcingle or roller, a one-time investment that will last forever with good care. It is possible to attach side reins to the girth provided you take care in adjusting the height. If your budget cannot stretch to both cavesson and surcingle, buy the cavesson.

The cavesson is fitted over the bridle but the nosepiece needs to be adjusted underneath the cheeks of the bridle to avoid interference with the action of the

The lungeing cavesson should be fastened underneath the cheek pieces so that you do not interfere with the pressure on the bit.

A correct cavesson has a jowl strap to prevent the cavesson being pulled to one side or the other. It should fasten under the jaw. Note: Some horses have such wide jawbones that this is impossible to do; in this case, make it as snug as you can. The reins should be twisted up and caught by this strap so the horse cannot trip over them.

bit. The lunge line attaches to the front ring of the nosepiece which is fitted tightly so it does not slip. Lungeing from a headcollar is of little value as the lunge line pulls the headcollar out of place and affords very little control.

I buckle the surcingle over the saddle, or over a saddle pad; it has buckles set at various heights for the side reins. I usually set the side reins so that when the horse is stretched forward to a contact with the bit, the mouth is level with the point of the horse's shoulder, with the nose in front of the vertical. I use all leather or fixed side reins, not the type with an elastic inset or rubber rings set halfway down the length. The reason for this is that the vast majority of horses

The surcingle fitted over the saddle with the side reins and overchecks loosely adjusted—not forcing the horse into a fixed position.

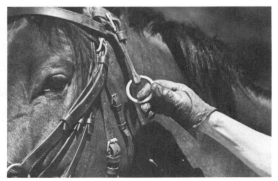

The rings for the overchecks. These are removable for when lungeing the rider.

will not pull against something fixed. Once they have tried to lean and found that the reins do not give, they relax the jaw to lessen the pressure on the bars of the mouth, whereas they can learn to lean on elastic side reins. However, I hasten to add that this rule is not inflexible. I have a horse in my barn who throws a fit in fixed reins but goes kindly in elastic ones; you have to study each horse as an individual.

In addition to the side reins I attach two overcheck reins running from buckles on the top of the surcingle through rings fastened to straps above the browband and down to the rings of the bit. The overchecks prevent the horse from leaning down on the bit and prevent it from coming behind the vertical. *They must not be tightly adjusted:* they are not used to raise the head, but to prevent it from being too low.

I was dubious about the overchecks at first, having learned several other ways of lungeing earlier. The benefits gained for all horses seem to be that the horses do not lean on their shoulders, but find a nice horizontal balance and stretch confidently to the bit without locking the muscles under the neck.

For horses that have rigid backs and go with their heads in the air, hollow with dragging hindquarters, it is better to lunge them at first without side reins, overchecks, or even a saddle. I use the cavesson only and keep the horse on a smallish (15 meter) circle at a steady trot. I wait until the horse reaches forward and down with the head and neck, thus stretching the back muscles. This only works if the horse keeps moving forward with a steady rhythm and not just fast with short quick steps. The horse must stretch the tight muscles on top of the spine.

It is wise to tie up the stirrups so they don't flap on the horse's sides and startle it.

This stretching work takes patience and time, perhaps as long as a month. As the horse stretches forward, the hindquarters begin to come under the body and the horse develops some swing and suspension. The stretching forward must be coupled with active steps; otherwise, the horse might just run along on the forehand. Swinging, bouncy steps behind are what you are after, with complete

A inexpensive substitute for lungeing equipment: a western bosal with a ring fixed in front. Heavy twine is used for the overcheck and a leather browband to hold the overcheck.

freedom of the spine. Once you have achieved a stretched, swinging trot, the horse can be lunged normally.

To start a horse on the lunge work, either a young horse or one that has never been lunged, I try to have someone to help me for the first two or three sessions. I also find an enclosed space. If you go out into an open field, you have little hope of holding onto a horse that decides to take off. In an enclosed space you can run the horse into the wall or fence, but in the open you are powerless. If it is not possible to find an indoor school or a small enclosure, use your ingenuity and create your own. Poles laid on top of barrels are better than nothing, cavaletti set in a circle will suffice, or you can create a circle of sorts with jump poles and standards. Perhaps two corners of a field can be enclosed with poles or even ropes tied to standards. Try to use something substantial so the horse will be reluctant to charge through your barrier.

An enclosed lungeing ring is useful but I actually prefer to have more space available, with the ideal being a small indoor or outdoor ring. Here you have the option of three 20-meter circles, one at each end and one in the middle, and also have the use of a straight line down the side.

For the first session with the young horse we tack up in the stall and let the horse feel all the various straps swinging around its sides. The horse is then led to the lungeing enclosure. The overchecks are fastened to the rings at the browband but not attached to the bit for the first sessions. One step at a time.

The side reins are fastened loosely to the bit without any pressure. Since most horses are "left-handed," it is best to start with a left-handed circle. The assistant stands on the outside of the circle with a hand on the rein, or a lead rope attached to the outside ring of the cavesson, while the trainer takes a stand in the middle of the circle with the lunge line and the lunge whip. The trainer says "Walk On!", cracks the whip gently, and the assistant starts forward (you need a well trained assistant!). The horse will usually go along because it is used to being led. After a circle or two, the trainer then says "Whoa" and the assistant and horse

Step one. The trainer is in charge and the assistant is ready to walk forward with the horse to show it the correct response to the voice and the lunge whip.

halt. Reward the horse with a pat. After a few turns around the circle with the assistant, the horse should have an idea of what you expect and should be ready to go on alone. Have your assistant drop the lead rope or the rein and, as the horse is walking on the circle, the assistant should move off to one side and stop. If the horse also stops, urge it on with your voice and the whip. After the horse has successfully made a circle solo, halt, praise it, and send it on again. If this is successful make a big fuss of the horse, give it some sugar, a piece of carrot or apple and "lots of pats" and *put it away for the day*. Remember, one step at a time, one new lesson per day is enough, particularly with the young horse. The brain of a young horse can absorb one thing at a time, so don't overload the circuit.

The next day start again with your assistant for the first circle, then get the horse revolving around you by itself. Next you need the horse to understand that it can also do this in the opposite direction. Begin the same way, this time to the right, with your assistant's help if needed, until the horse can make circles around you in both directions.

The next step is teaching the horse to go forward. To me, this is *the* most important lunge lesson: the horse must go forward immediately upon command. Use a sharp voice command "Trot on!" or "Ter-rot" and crack the whip. If the horse ignores you, use the lash on the hindquarters and chase it on. It does not matter if the horse canters at this point; let it, send it forward and keep it going. The rhythm will probably be erratic, the balance horrible, but keep sending that horse forward. *Forward first.*

The excitable horse may well fly around you, stumble and even fall over but keep sending it forward; it will soon learn to put its feet underneath itself and keep upright. These sessions can become quite alarming but persevere; let the horse figure things out for itself.

On the other hand you may face a horse that flatly refuses to budge. Here you need your trusty assistant again. Position the assistant on the outside of the circle with a second lunge whip. If you are in an indoor ring, the assistant needs to become the "fourth wall" in the open part of the ring. If you have only a circle, the assistant needs to be in a position to use the whip on the horse's hindquarter. You chase the horse from the inside while the assistant chases from the outside until the horse gets the message.

This can be an exhausting exercise for everyone, but don't give up until you get that horse moving forward.

We once had a young colt who planted all four feet and refused to move one step, then threw himself over backwards rather than go foward. It took the united efforts of myself and two other people armed with whips to get him to go. We all got lashed by each other during the process, we were out of breath and scarlet-faced by the time we finished and the horse was wringing wet, but he lunged perfectly everafter.

These battles are certainly not the norm but they do occur. If they do, you must be prepared to stay at it until you win. A young horse that has been treated with too much deference by doting owners, as was the case with the colt, can be difficult when first asked to work for a living, as well as dangerous to itself and you. I love horses but I expect them to toe the line and to produce when asked. They are altogether too big and too powerful to be allowed to push people around.

The initial lessons on the lunge serve to get the horse moving freely forward in trot and canter. As soon as it can do this, you can begin to shorten the side reins, hole by hole, and do up the overchecks. I do not do much work in the walk in the early stages because the average horse tends to drag around anyway. I keep both overchecks at the same length, and tighten them only so they come

This horse is moving forward but is hollow. He needs to keep working until he stretches the neck forward and down, and brings his back up under the saddle.

into play if the horse puts its head down below the point of the shoulders. I set the inner side rein two holes shorter than the outside one. This gives an indication of bending and helps the horse stretch to the outside rein. You want the horse to be stretched and well balanced from back to front, not to shorten the neck artificially. The horse must learn to bring its hindlegs well up under its belly and to arch its topline.

The circle is the basis for all dressage work; keep the horse on a circle long enough and it will begin to go correctly.

Often the horse will have difficulty finding its balance in the canter on a circle. If it falls back to the trot, send it on again. Each time it performs a canter depart, it has to bring the hindlegs up under the body and the canter will begin to be better balanced. If the horse cross canters (leads with one leg in front and the other behind), send it on and try to send it close to the wall or the fence. It will usually switch back to a true canter because the horse will be reluctant to carry its hindlegs against the wall and will change in self defense.

For the horse that really rushes around the circle, my advice at this point is to let it. If you try to pacify it, you are creating a conflict. If the horse wants to run, let it until it finds that there is no percentage in running. When it has run around enough to get tired and begins to break down to the trot, send it on again in canter: *let it be your idea to canter this time.* This is more effective than picking an argument. If you do not fight the forward impulse, which is really an evasion, the horse will eventually realize that running gets it nowhere. If, on the other hand, you keep trying to stop the horse, isn't that really what it wants, not to work? I admit it took me a long time to figure that out.

Always lunge in both directions, first to the left, then to the right, making the proper adjustments to the side reins. After about two or three weeks, you should be ready to start some real work on the lunge.

Up to this point you have been lungeing on a standard 20-meter circle. Now you can begin to decrease and increase the size of the circle. Bring the horse in

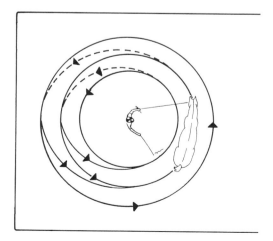

First variation: making the circle smaller, then larger to engage the hindlegs.

towards you by shortening the lunge line and then let it drift out again to the original circle. This is particularly good for horses that stay strung out behind; the smaller circle makes them bend and engage. At first don't insist on more than one small circle. As the horse's balance improves, you can keep it longer on the smaller circle. If you want to work the canter, use the same exercise. You can use frequent transitions to halt and forward again. This, in particular, works well on horses with rigid backs: the act of halting and moving off again forces them to shift balance and helps free up the hindlegs. In fact, transitions are the key to shifting the horse's weight from front to back. The horse on its forehand creeps into downward transitions because all its weight keeps rolling forward. By making it stop and go forward again, you develop more thrust from behind. So practice downward transitions and upward transitions with regularity.

I try to keep the lunge work varied which is why I prefer more room than a lungeing pen offers. I work up and down the sides of the school, working a circle at one end, then letting the horse go straight down the side, then working a middle circle with no support from the walls, and then moving to the far end of the school for a third circle.

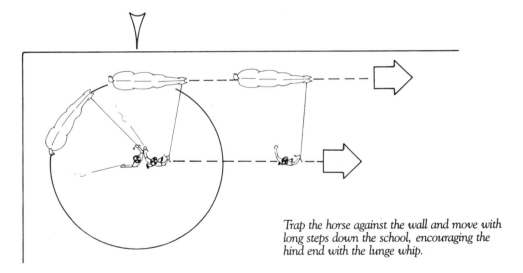

Trap the horse against the wall and move with long steps down the school, encouraging the hind end with the lunge whip.

Once the horse is balanced and moving with good rhythm on the lunge, you can teach it to lengthen its stride. Position yourself on the quarter line of the arena, and have the horse trot on a 10-meter circle around you. As the horse approaches the wall, start to move down the school yourself, trapping the horse against the wall so it leaves the circle and travels straight. If the horse breaks into canter, which it may well do, stop moving and guide it back onto the 10-meter circle. As you make your move down the school, try to run with long floating strides yourself so that the horse can pick up on your body language. With a little practice you will find that the horse will give you a definite lengthening of

The horse is moving well on the circle, "held" by the two corners of the fence.

Make a move straight ahead. Here, the trainer is actually a little too far ahead of the horse; she should be level with its shoulders. The horse is already reaching out.

Keep on pushing down the wall.

The horse is pushing well from behind—look at the right hind leg stepping under.

Don't be greedy; be satisfied with some good steps. Then slow up and bring the horse back onto a circle around you.

the stride with engagement from behind and pronounced suspension, exactly what you want instead of a mere rushing. This applies to the canter as well, but you must be able to move yourself down the school nimbly for this—not all of us can run that fast!

Daily lungeing pays off in the training of any horse. Far from being a boring exercise of just watching your horse go in circles, the horse is developing muscles, balance and rhythm before you ever get on. If you lunge first, when you get on your horse it is ready to work and you do not need a 20-minute warmup period. You have allowed your horse to work its initial freshness out of its system, you have let it loosen up the muscles, and you have channeled its energy into constructive forward impulse. Now you can begin whatever work you have in mind for the day.

For the rider

If you have been fortunate enough to watch a performance by the riders of the Spanish Riding School of Vienna, you must have been struck by the ease and elegance of their positions in the saddle. Without exception they sit quietly, molded to their horses even in the difficult airs above the ground. How did they develop those immaculate positions? *On the lunge line.* Apprentice riders at the school spend from *three to six months* on a horse on the lunge line before they are allowed to touch the reins. To be in control of a horse you must be in control of your own body.

Work on the lunge is the fastest, most effective way to develop a correct seat. It may be boring, but it works.

The equipment you need is a well schooled quiet horse, lunging cavesson, side reins, and a well designed deep seated saddle. Trying to develop a deep seat on a postage stamp-sized forward seat saddle is an exercise in futility and excruciatingly uncomfortable to boot. You also need a patient friend or instructor.

All men and women are not created equal, unfortunately, and your final position in the saddle will be dictated by your basic shape. We would all like to be tall with long elegant legs but, with work, even those with short rounded legs can achieve a balanced seat that is functional. The key to a good position is balance, not strength, and balance comes from aligning the various parts of your body so that they are in harmony and supple enough to absorb the horse's movement. Just sitting pretty isn't enough, you must be functional.

First, we must analyze how the horse moves under us, in order to accommodate our own body to each movement. With that in mind, let's examine the correct position for the rider.

As we have seen, no part of the horse's weight lies on top of its spine so any move you make with your upper body above the saddle drastically affects the horse's balance. You need to be able to sit in the middle of your horse with the upper body lined up in the center.

Your head needs to be turned in the direction of movement without tilting. Your eyes should always be looking in the direction the horse is moving. There is a good reason for this: the head is the largest and heaviest single bone in your

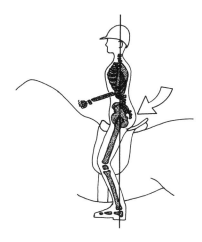

The rider's hip and pelvic joint are the connection to the horse's spine and transmit many different signals, provided the rider's balance is good.

body and whatever you do with it can be felt by your horse. Rightly or wrongly, the horse will learn to follow the weight as it shifts. Your shoulders need to stay parallel to the line of the horse's shoulders and be relaxed and open. Your arms, and therefore your hands, begin at the shoulders and any tenseness there will be transmitted directly to the horse's mouth.

Your spine should be stretched from the waist up, carrying the two upper "blocks," the shoulders and head, and the torso comfortably. Your hips should be relaxed, with your legs dropping from the hip to wrap around the horse's sides. The more you can relax your hip joint, the longer your leg will hang and you will be able to sit "into" your horse instead of merely perching on top of it. Gripping tightly with the knee is counterproductive because it limits the use of your lower leg. If you grip tightly, the horse will contract the muscles under the saddle

The leg must drop from the hip so that your weight falls down into your heels and your feet support your body.

If you grip tightly with the knee, the heels come up and the lower leg becomes ineffective; the horse will stiffen. Frequently, the rider's body will fall forward.

and become more rigid and heavy in your hand. You do not want to be flip-flopping all over your horse but to stretch and cling. The German saying is "Your leg should wrap around the horse like a piece of wet cloth." There is nothing rigid about a piece of wet cloth, but it clings.

Imagine your body divided into three blocks: the head and shoulders, the torso, the pelvis and legs. You want to balance these blocks on top of each other as your horse begins to move. It is easy to sit on a stationary horse and look good, but what happens when you get into motion?

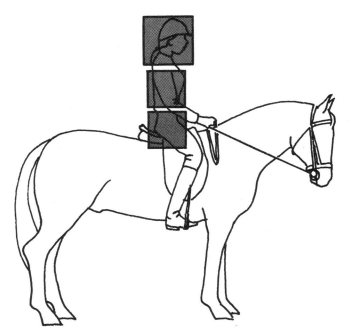

The balanced blocks of the correct position.

In the walk, the horse's movement is regular and slow. The spine undulates both up and down and from side to side. Each leg moves independently but in a diagonal sequence: right front, left hind, left front, right hind. Think of the walk as being a diagonal movement with broken diagonals. As the hind leg swings forward the barrel sways to the opposite side. Encourage this sway by using your own leg to roll with it and your horse will reach out and march forward.

In the trot, however, things get more complicated. The horse moves its legs in diagonal pairs: right front and left hind, left front and right hind, with a moment of suspension in between. The horse's shoulder blades swing back and forth in that great cradle of supporting muscles, but the key to the trot lies behind the saddle, where the hips of the horse swing up and down as the hindlegs bend and step under the body. The spine, as we discussed earlier, runs right through the pelvic joint and is directly effected by the up and down movement of the horse's hips. The result is that the spine develops a little rock and roll of its own. If you grip tightly to keep your seat in the saddle, trying to absorb the motion, you prevent the spine from swinging freely. If you bump about, your horse will hollow its back in self defense. The trick to sitting the trot is to absorb the roll

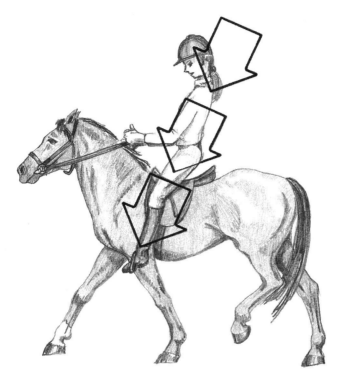

Bumping on the horse's back will not allow the horse to move comfortably; you need to sit "with" the motion. If the rider is rigid on the spine, the horse will lock its back in self defense.

in your own hip joint and spine. You can do this by sitting on one seat bone, then the other, in time to the horse's trot. Sounds complicated? Let's analyze it further.

When you ride in posting trot, you rise out of the saddle when the horse's outside front leg swings forward—on the outside diagonal, in other words. Why? Probably because your first instructor told you to. But *why?* When the outside foreleg swings forward so does the inside hind. When the horse is on a circle or curve, the inside hind has to bend slightly more than the outside hind which has to reach more. When you *rise* out of the saddle with the *outside foreleg*, you are freeing up the *inside hind* so it can bend more easily without your added weight on it.

In the trot, the horse's legs move in diagonal pairs. You ride the posting trot by lifting out of the saddle on the outside front leg to free the inside leg.

When you sit the trot, you must drop to the inside as the outside front leg moves forward so that you are sitting with the inside hind.

When you sit to the trot, you need to sit *with* that inside hind in order to absorb the roll of the spine to that side. So you weight the *inside seatbone* as the *outside foreleg* swings forward: left seatbone as the right fore swings, right seatbone as the left fore swings.

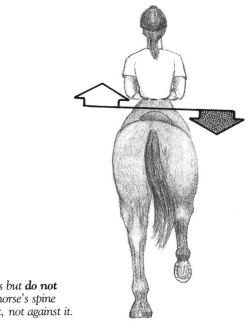

Follow the motion with your hips but **do not** drop your shoulders. Allow the horse's spine to swing freely by moving with it, not against it.

Warning: this movement must be imperceptible to anyone on the ground; don't get carried away and start tilting your shoulders. I once taught a group of riders to follow the movement and came back three months later to find them all tipping from side to side with their horses becoming more and more unbalanced. The easiest lesson I ever gave, on the other hand, was in Hawaii, when they all said "Oh, just like doing the hula!" And so it is, you do it all with the hips.

Once you master this balance and motion, you will find all horses become easier to sit. To those people who tell me their horse has a "horrible sitting trot," I can only say, "No. Your horse has locked its back. Free up the spine and show the horse you can move with it and the trot becomes more comfortable immediately."

Understanding the motion of the horse's spine gives you a great advantage when it comes to riding transitions. To move from trot to walk, or to a halt, if you are sitting properly and moving with the horse's back, all you have to do is just stop the action of your spine and hip. The horse will walk or halt, depending upon how strong you make your action. You are sitting on the central nervous system, the main line to the brain. The horse can feel anything you do up

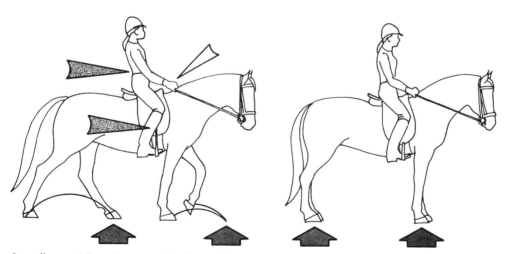

In walk, you follow the swing of the horse's barrel from side to side using your legs alternately. To halt, close both legs together and stop the action of your hips. Then close your fingers on the rein. The horse will stop from behind and step up squarely to the front. Legs–Seat–Hands—in that order.

there. "Brace your back" is the usual phrase you hear, but I prefer to say "Stop your back action for a moment." You then get a transition that begins with the horse's hindquarters; the horse does not fall on its forehand or dive down onto the bit because you have not offered it the option to do so. You get a prompt, forward transition with no loss of balance. You get trot-walk, not trot-stop-walk. And "Look Ma, no hands!" If you can do this on the lunge, you will be well on your way to riding good transitions when you get your reins back.

If the rider's weight is forward, the horse falls into downward transitions instead of engaging the hindquarter and stepping under itself.

To make the transition from trot to walk, be sure you are following the motion of the horse's spine with your hips. To walk, just stop that motion and close your fingers. Immediately pick up the swing of the walk with your body. Give the aids to make the transition and then allow the horse to do it. Don't hang on as your aids then turn into driving forward aids.

In the canter the horse has yet another motion, and its legs move in a different pattern. In the left lead canter, for instance, the horse starts the canter with the right hind moving up under the body, taking the entire support of the horse and rider. This leg provides the thrust of the canter stride. The right fore and left hind rotate forward and "catch" the weight to balance it, while the leading leg, the left fore, is actually the last leg to touch down. Then all four feet come off the ground for a split second and the cycle repeats.

As the horse's inside hind and outside fore swing forward, its spine rises under the rider's inside seat bone and then drops away. The spine also has a tendency to flex to the outside. To follow the movement the rider needs to swing the inside hip bone towards the pommel of the saddle with a forward rotation. This allows the inside hind to swing up under the belly. Actually, you want to ride the canter with the small of your back and a flexible spine. The outside leg of the rider should remain slightly behind the girth and "massage" the horse's side in unison with the inside leg at the girth.

Since the horse's motion and the rider's motion at the canter are different from the trot, the timing and motion for the downward transition also differs. Given the sequence of the canter, it stands to reason that the moment at which the horse can rearrange its feet and come down in a different pattern is the moment when all four feet are in the air. So you need to give the aid *immediately before the moment of suspension*, when the leading leg swings forward. In other words, if you ask for a transition when the leading leg comes to the ground, the next instant the horse has all its legs in the air and can easily change to trot, walk, halt, or perform a flying change. How do you achieve this?

Since you are sitting on your inside seatbone and following the motion of the inside hind (and outside fore) with your back, you must establish the moment that the leading leg comes down. Try saying "now – now – now," each time the leading leg swings forward. You will find that it happens when you are actively swinging your inside hip towards the pommel. As the leading leg comes down, shift your weight quickly to the outside seatbone. What have you done? You have transferred your weight from the inside hind leg to the outside hind leg just as it is going into the air to begin the next canter sequence. In effect, you have blocked it. The horse cannot take the next canter step but, instead, "grounds" the outside hind and comes down in trot, or walk if your timing is good and the horse really well balanced. Eventually you will be able to achieve canter to halt with the same aid. If your timing is good, you will be amazed by the response of even a green horse. In the transition to trot, you need to pick up the movement of the trot *immediately* in your hip joint.

Usually green horses are on the forehand in the transition from canter to trot and fall into a running shamble until the rider recovers. By riding the transition from the hind leg, the horse flows from one gait to the next without the interim panic. The same timing applies later on to flying changes.

All the work you do on understanding the horse's movement in the early stages will pay off handsomely in later training, when it is vital to know where each leg is at every moment in order to influence it. To be able to control your own actions this precisely, you must work at your position and stretch your muscles to reduce any difficulties.

I have a whole set of exercises, each more satanic than the other, that will lead you to perfect control and relaxation. But don't ever think that riding is easy, because there is no substitute for time and hard work.

All of the following exercises can be performed at the walk, trot and eventually at the canter. You should practice first at the walk until you have control over your own limbs, then graduate to the trot and later the canter. It takes time to achieve all this, but those who have taken gymnastics or ballet will have better control over their bodies and will progress faster than those who are not as limber. For clarity's sake, we show these exercises with the rider "solo," but keep in mind the benefits of working on the lunge.

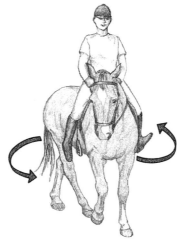

Exercise One: For the ankles. Rotate your feet and ankles by dropping your toes, circling them to the sides and up again. Work clockwise, then counterclockwise.

Exercise Two: For the leg and hip joint. Swing your leg from the hip joint back and forth along the sides of the horse (be careful not to kick it). Work on getting a supple movement with a straight knee; don't just kick from a bent knee, move the entire leg, thigh and all. Swing one leg backwards, one forwards. Stretch back as far as you can.

Exercise Three: For the thigh. Take hold of one ankle with your hand on the same side and stretch your thigh back as far as possible. Don't force it but try to get your knee as far back as possible. When you have done this on both sides separately, do both legs together. When you release the ankle, let the leg fall into place without moving the knee forward. You will find you are already deeper in the saddle.

Exercise Four: For the hip joint (the real killer). Point your toes out sideways and lift your knees up and out until they are level with the pommel. Hold as long as you can, then relax the leg down. This exercise will pinpoint your stiffness in the hip joint; you will probably feel a real pinch in the hip muscles. Don't force this exercise, just do what is comfortable and relax, gradually working up to where you can hold the leg up for a count of twenty. Both legs need to work together. When you can successfully do this at the canter, you are really supple!

Exercise Five: For the waist and torso. Place your hands on your hips and turn as far to each side as you can while keeping your head to the front.

Exercise Six: Also for waist and shoulders. With arms at shoulder height, swing them from side to side keeping your head facing front.

Exercise Seven: For waist and upper body. Raise your arms above your head with palms facing, stretching up as much as possible. Turn from the waist, first to one side, then the other, while maintaining the stretch.

Exercise Eight: For waist and upper body. Raise your arms above the head beginning with palms facing. Let one arm circle forwards, the other one backwards. This takes both concentration and coordination but really supples your waist and the small of your back. Try to get a good swing from the top with your arms falling down like pendulums. After you master it, reverse the direction of the arms: if you began with the left swinging back and the right forward, now swing the left forward and the right back.

Exercise Nine: For the shoulders. Place your hands on your shoulders and rotate your elbows backwards, then forward, in a circular motion.

Exercise Ten: For the arms and hands. Hold your arms straight out in front of you and touch your fingertips together one at a time. Start with your thumbs uppermost, touch your thumbs, first fingers, second fingers and so. This will help you separate your arm and hand movements from the rest of the body, which is all important if you are to develop a fine control of the rein actions.

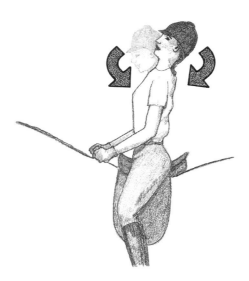

Exercise Eleven: For the head and shoulders. Drop your head as far back as you can, roll it around to the side and let it drop forward. Don't lean over or shift from side to side. This is a balance-improving exercise.

Exercise Twelve: For the arms. Hold your arms out in front of you and pretend you are punching a punching bag. Use each arm alternately, punching upwards, out to the side, and downwards.

All of these exercises can easily be done on the ground. Another good exercise is to stand on the bottom step of a flight of stairs, a cinder block, or anything a few inches off the ground, and hang your heels over the edge, doing deep knee bends while keeping your body upright. This gives you the control you need when your weight comes correctly down into your stirrups.

For those who have trouble in keeping their legs under their body when mounted, I recommend riding rising trot, then remaining up in the rising position for an entire circle. You may need to grab mane with one hand to pull yourself up, but there is a definite point of balance you will find. Once you find it, like riding a bicycle, you have it for good. If you grip too tightly with your knee in this exercise, you will be unable to support your upper body; relax the knee and bounce off your ankle joint. The balance here is exactly the same as in skiing over bumps.

Remember, balance, not strength, is the key to a deep, secure, supple position.

◇ 3 ◇
THE WORK IN HAND

The practice of working the horse in hand dates back to the great masters of the art but seems to have fallen into neglect in many countries, perhaps because not many modern trainers learn the skill. As with lungeing, work in hand is not intended as a substitute for mounted training but can serve as a useful extension of the work under saddle. Work in hand gives the horse a chance to redistribute its weight without the added burden of the rider. It also accustoms the horse to the use of the whip, and is of great value in instilling respect for the trainer's authority.

For work in hand you do not need any special equipment beyond the bridle and a long dressage whip.

The young horse at the start of training needs at least a month or so of muscle building before you begin any serious work in hand. Once the horse can be lunged in walk, trot and canter in both directions, you can begin. For the older horse undergoing retraining, the work in hand can begin at any time.

This type of work brings the young horse to obedience and teaches it to distribute its weight correctly. For the older, spoiled horse, the work in hand is of value for stretching and bending the all important joints of the hind legs. Above all, the work in hand shows the horse the way to the outside rein and teaches the balance and roundness needed for collected work.

After lungeing the horse, take off the lungeing surcingle, the side reins and the overchecks. At first, leave the cavesson on over the bridle and attach a short lead rope in place of the lunge line. If you run into difficulty in the first lesson you certainly don't need all that lunge line in your hand and, since you want to avoid using the reins and abusing the horse's mouth, the short lead rope makes it easier to correct or hold the horse if it misbehaves.

As with the lunge work, start your work in hand to the left, unless your horse is decidedly "right-handed." Place yourself by the horse's left shoulder, facing forward, and take the left rein and the lead rope in your left hand a few inches from the bit. Hold the whip in your right hand like a fencing foil and take hold of the right rein over the wither, placing your hand behind the girth where your

Leave the cavesson on over the bridle and attach a short lead rope. Stand by the horse's shoulder facing forward. With the leading hand, in this example the left hand, hold the left rein close to the bit along with the lead rope. The right hand should be positioned just about where your left heel would be if you were mounted and holds the whip horizontally with the right rein across the wither.

left leg would normally rest. Your left hand will control the head, your right hand will control the shoulders, and the whip will act on the hindquarters.

A whip can be used for different reasons: it can be used to instruct or to correct, with varying degrees of sharpness. It is up to you as trainer to use the whip when necessary with the needed amount of strength. When you are teaching a new lesson, the whip serves to instruct and should be used tactfully and gently. Use it as lightly as possible to make the horse displace a leg in the desired direction. On the other hand, when the horse resists or kicks out against the whip, it must be sharply reprimanded and hit quickly and sharply.

Exercise One: This exercise will teach the horse to accept the touch of the whip and to move forward promptly from a slight touch. Standing beside the horse facing its head, reach back and touch the left hind leg, close to the hock. If the horse picks up the leg and steps forward, praise it and repeat. If the horse crosses the left hind in front of the right hind, praise it again. However, if the horse kicks out irritably against the whip, use a ferocious voice and hit it sharply

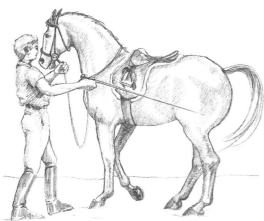

Exercise One and Three. *Tap the horse on the hind leg until it picks it up and moves it away from you.*

in the same place to let it know that kicking out is undesirable. Repeat the action with the whip. If the horse kicks again, hit it again, and keep this up until the horse stops kicking and moves away from the touch.

The horse may fly away from the touch of the whip. Be elastic in your arms and move with it. There is no way you can hold 1,000 pounds or so of nervous horse effectively, so move towards it and hold onto the lead rope so that the horse cannot escape you. Once you have the horse back under control repeat the action of the whip. Keep at it until the horse accepts.

Move to the other side of the horse and go through the same steps. All these exercises must be done on both sides of the horse.

Exercise Two. *Once the horse moves forward from a tap on the croup, that is, activates the hindquarter from a touch of the whip, walk forward and circle to the left.*

Exercise Two: Touch the horse on top of the croup and draw it forward on a small circle. Walk with it, making much of it with your voice and patting it when you stop. Once the horse is comfortable with the use of the whip on the leg and on the croup, you can begin to build up your repetoire of lessons.

Exercise Three: Stand facing the horse with your left hand close to the bit, and your right hand holding the rein that crosses the wither and the whip. With the whip, ask the horse to step around you sideways, crossing front and hind legs. The horse will perform a version of a turn on the forehand but on a slightly larger radius.

Exercise Four. *Positioned for the work in the shoulder-in. The horse is angled from the fence to prevent the hindquarter from escaping away from the trainer.*

Exercise Four: After mastering exercise three, you can begin to ask for some steps of shoulder-in down the long side of the school or along the fence. The wall serves to control the hindquarters which otherwise might swing away from you out of control. Tap the horse on the hindleg and move your body towards it down the track of the arena. Ask the horse to bend around your body and step sideways away from you. Take one or two steps like this, then step forward onto a small cricle. The horse should be curved around you, stepping towards the right rein while the left side should be soft and relaxed.

If you let the wall hold the hindquarters, the horse has to bend its spine and yield. Prevent the horse from walking forward into the arena with the right, or outside rein. The left, or inside rein, holds a soft contact, just enough to control the position of the head. Once they understand this exercise, most horses will readily soften the muscles of the neck on the inside. You are creating the correct

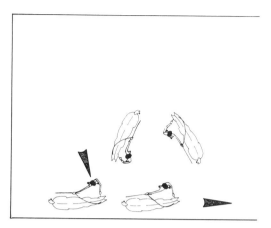

Ask for one or two steps, then allow the horse to walk forward onto the circle, and ask again for the shoulder-in.

Exercise Four, more advanced. The horse crosses front and hind legs, and moves smoothly with a light elastic contact on the rein. Here, there is too much bend in the neck. Once the horse understands this exercise, it can be performed anywhere. But in the beginning, use the rail or wall to help control the hindquarters.

response and teaching the horse to accept the bit. Don't try and hold the horse in position by force; the horse must learn to relax and carry itself. The reins should remain light and elastic, and the horse must not lean on your hand.

Take your time teaching this shoulder-in exercise. Work in hand can be awkward for both horse and trainer at first. You will find that your arms ache and the horse may not understand the demand. But when you are comfortable with this exercise and the horse remains light, calm, and moves in a steady rhythm, the succeeding exercises will fall into place.

Again, once you have worked the left side, switch and work to the right. It may seem like an entirely new ballgame: just because the horse has accepted you on the left does not necessarily mean it will accept you on the right. In fact, since most horses have more difficulty to the right, you may well find it is like starting all over. Persevere.

If the horse offers a great deal of resistance, or insists on walking right on top of you, you may have to resort to using the butt end of the whip on its shoulder. The horse must respect your space, and move away from you, not running you down, or running through your hand. It can be a struggle in the early stages, and your first attempt with the horse can take some time. Don't hesitate to use your voice to admonish the horse; berate it if it resists (develop a good growl), sound furious but don't lose your temper—just sound as if you have. Be equally quick to use a soothing voice if the horse so much as gives an indication of trying to do what you ask. Any long drawn out vowel sound seems to work "Aaaaah. Oooooh. Gooood." I use the word "Braaaav" much of the time, mainly because I have had European teachers, but any noise is fine as long as it is soothing. Horses cannot talk but they hear well. Remember how instinctive the horse is, that any correction or praise needs to be instantaneous if the horse is to associate it with an action. I cannot stress this enough. If the horse is to realize its actions are wrong, you must correct it immediately, and if it is to realize its actions are correct, you must stop and praise at once. The horse's instinct and reflexes are those of an animal, and twice as fast as ours. If you can train yourself to become as instinctive as your horse, you will be well on the road to successful training.

When teaching new skills, don't belabor the point. Five minutes or so daily will bring you and your horse to a built-up confidence in each other. After a week to ten days, you should be able to walk in shoulder-in all around your arena on both reins. As with any work, it is the daily repetition that enables the horse to become trained. If you do this just once a week, each time you will have to start all over at the beginning.

Exercise Five: We can now begin to teach the half pass. Work your shoulder-in down the long side and guide the horse onto the center line. With the horse bent around you to the left, as you reach the center line pull down on the right rein across the wither, straighten your left arm, and push the horse's head away from you. You want the horse to shift its weight from left to right and to reverse the bend. Position yourself so that you step across the horse's chest and tap the hindquarters to send them away from the whip, asking the horse to go back to the wall in half pass. When you reach the wall, stop, loosen the rein and praise.

Exercise Five. *Push the head away to the far side of the shoulders. At the same time, push the hindquarters with a touch of the whip so the horse bends away from you. Most horses will react like this one: they stiffen and hollow out. Just continue to insist until the horse accepts the new demand. Remember, it is important to keep moving forward as well as sideways.*

This particular exercise can be confusing at first, but if you change the bend smoothly and quickly, coordinating your hands, then relaxing the rein pressure so you are not forcing the horse, it will accept the new concept. The fact that you asking the horse to step towards the security of the track is to your advantage. You can actually feel the horse shift its weight in this exercise and will begin to see some vestige of the hindquarters engaging, with the forehand becoming correspondingly light.

Take the time to become comfortable with both the shoulder-in and the half pass. You should be able to shift from one to the other without losing rhythm or creating resistance in the mouth. Steady and slow is the motto here, and make sure the horse stays relaxed.

Exercises Six and Seven: You can now begin to use the two previous exercises in more sophisticated patterns. Make a 15-meter circle in shoulder-in with you on the inside of the circle, with the horse's shoulders making a slightly larger track, the hindquarters moving outside the shoulders, and the hindlegs stepping under and across. Be sure to keep the steps even and regular.

When you reach a point in the middle of the school, change the bend as if for the half pass and describe a new circle with the horse bent away from you.

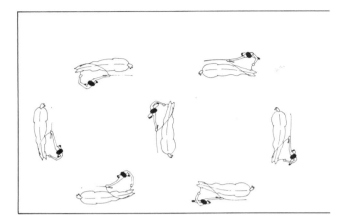

Excercises Six and Seven.
Peform a circle in shoulder-in.
Cross the center of the circle,
change the bend, and perform a
circle around the hindquarters
(a circle in half pass).

Now you are on the outside of the circle, the horse is bent away from you with the shoulders making a larger circle than the hindquarters. I find I have to increase the length of my own strides to be able to push the shoulders around. Take care that the horse still steps with the left hind leg crossing over in front of the

Excercise Eight. *It is amazing how far under and across the hind legs can step. This is terrific preparation for collected work. This exercise tends to make you very dizzy!*

right hind. This is more difficult for the horse on a circle than on a straight line, and brings greater engagement. Keep the size of the circle large at first to lessen the demands on the joints. The horse will step on its own feet if you try to make too small a circle at first or if you do not have enough forward motion. As the balance and suppleness increase, you can decrease the size of your rotations.

Exercise Eight: You can now ask for increased bending of the hindlegs. Position yourself beside the horse, facing the hindquarters. Hold the left rein with your arm stretched out to the side. Tap the horse on the hock and step towards the left hind. You want the horse to trot around you on a tiny circle. Tap the horse each time the left hind is about to leave the ground and make it step up and over the right hind. If you want the horse to bend the hip, stifle and hock joints, you can tap it on top of the croup. If you want it to cross over more, tap on the gaskin, just above the hock. It is amazing how far under the horse can reach. You will find once you get the hang of this exercise that your horse will develop a good rhythm and will actually increase its suspension. This exercise is a preparation for the piaffe later on. It is a strenuous exercise and you must be very careful not to overdo it. Let the horse build its agility and strength slowly. Build muscles; don't break them down.

Exercise Nine. *Don't force the horse backwards; the aim is to develop a swing back and forward again. Use your own body motion to show the horse what is required.*

Exercise Nine: Bring the horse to the wall and ask for some steps backwards and then walk forward an equal number of steps. Alternate forward and backwards steps. This builds the ability to shift onto the hindquarters and push forward with more collection and bending of the joints. Be sure the evenness of the steps remains throughout.

Build skills one by one; the time taken at the early stages will lead to excellent results later.

The work in hand can bring you to a better understanding of the use of rein aids and, with time, you will be able to see the shifts of weight the horse must make to perform various movements. This work will carry over into mounted work since the horse will have some understanding of the lateral movements.

◇4◇
THE BASIC WORK IN ALL THREE GAITS

It would be ideal if we could all start out with the perfect horse, one that has good conformation, good gaits and above all a good temperament. Today, however, the competition for such horses is so great that the financial requirements are beyond most of us. The challenge of dressage training is to work with what you have, or can afford, and improve it. You are not going to transform a 15 hand round quarter horse, a 14.2 arabian, or a long-backed thoroughbred-cross into an Ahlerich, but you can certainly transform each of them by changing the way it handles its weight and covers the ground. The goal is to make each horse perform the best it can, given its natural shape and way of going, and to make it "pleasant to ride."

The goal is the same for each horse, and the basic principles are classical in origin. But sometimes there is more than one road to the end result, and you must consider each horse as an individual, using various exercises to remedy particular problems. Most dressage books give you one option, presupposing you have excellent material to work with, but "it ain't necessarily so." I hope I can offer some useful tips for "one-horse" owners and trainers.

The foremost requirement for any horse is that it go forward freely on command. Sound simple? *The desire to move forward* is not inherent in all horses, but frequently has to be created by the rider. Without this forward desire, you have nothing—there is not much point to teaching any of the exercises until the horse understands it must go forward at all times. And going forward has nothing to do with speed.

By the time you have taught the horse to lunge, it should understand it must go forward when asked. Now it must also understand that concept when you are in the saddle.

I do not want to detail here how to break young horses, that is another subject entirely. Presumably your horse has been broken, has been in muscle-building work for at least a month, and is ready for serious training. The older horse who has been used for different purposes—racing, cutting, barrel racing, showing, hunting or whatever—also needs muscle tone. Dressage work is strenuous; a horse must have some degree of fitness before you start to reshape its body and mind.

For the early work I carry a long dressage whip and forego the use of spurs on the majority of horses because I believe the horse needs to go from your leg alone. But there are horses that just will not respond to a light leg action and for those I make an exception and use spurs from the beginning. My reasoning here is that spurs are a refinement of the aids, not a replacement. Later on in advanced work, you will need spurs and it is good to have the option of using them then. If the horse is dull to the leg, it can become equally dull to the spur. You must make the decision with each horse.

I use a loose ring snaffle for most horses. Horses that have the tendency to roll their tongue around, or open their mouth too wide to avoid contact with the bit, may need a dropped or flash noseband. However, I prefer to work without these restraints if at all possible. If you tie the horse's mouth shut at the beginning of training, you run the risk of making it set its jaw and developing a rigid mouth. The horse will then contract the muscles throughout its entire body.

For advanced training I put the horse into a double bridle. Again, there is no set rule; it all depends on the individual horse. Horses that have learned to lean on the snaffle can often be reschooled in a double bridle and then returned to the snaffle with excellent results. In general, the less bit and restraint you use, the better.

If the horse has been lunged in side reins it is already used to a contact with the bit, so you can start right away to hold an elastic feel on both reins. When you mount, make the horse stand still while you pick up the reins and establish a light contact with the mouth. This is an important discipline; too many riders let the horse move off as soon as they get on and then pick up the reins. I believe the horse must stand still until you are completely ready to move forward. After

The horse should relax the jaw and poll,
and be ready to move forward promptly.

all, the first move in a dressage test is an immobile halt; why not condition the horse to be obedient from the beginning?

Wait until the horse accepts the rein and relaxes the jaw. Some horses will fuss at the contact, but just stay flexible in your arm and nudge them with your legs; don't let them move off. Some try to avoid contact by dropping the bit; again, use your leg and hold a contact. Some horses will stand with a rigid jaw and lean on your hand; just wait it out. A horse will rarely pull against a fixed rein, and if you keep the feel until the horse relaxes its jaw and then relax your own muscles, you are building the correct response. When the horse gives, you give; don't drop the contact, just soften your arm muscles. As soon as you get the

The lesson of the leg. The horse must move promptly forward from a light squeeze given with your entire leg, a fraction behind the girth. It should be a forward movement, with the weight in your heels pushing the horse forward. Relax immediately after tightening. If the horse ignores you, or resists, repeat and reinforce with a sharp tap of the whip.

response of softening, press your legs into the horse's side by the girth and ask it to move forward with a soft jaw. Don't go forward until you get softness.

Your legs should be close to the girth on both sides and should squeeze, then immediately relax. If you give a long drawn-out aid, the horse may tighten its muscles against the leg and not respond. By giving the aid and then relaxing, the horse has nothing to resist. You want the horse to step forward with a steady head and to go freely into walk or trot. If the horse does move promptly forward, pat it.

If, on the other hand, the horse ignores the leg, tap it with your whip at the girth to reinforce the aid. If the horse then plunges forward, let it go a few steps before you stop it. You just asked it to go forward and that is the important command; don't confuse the horse by immediately stopping even if it goes too fast. Let the lesson sink in. Don't say "Go!" and "Stop!" in the same breath.

The first lessons of the leg are all important and set the stage for all future training, so it pays to have the horse understand thoroughly.

Some horses are really thick—thick skinned and thick headed—and it can take a week or so before they really understand they must go forward. I had a young horse in for training and during the first two weeks I rode him, every time

The horse should step actively forward from the leg and remain on a soft contact.

This horse has hollowed as he stepped forward. Allow a couple of steps, then repeat the halt and move off again until the horse remains relaxed.

I got off I was quite exhausted, feeling as if I had taken every step for him. I almost put on spurs to galvanize him into action; I hit him every other step just to get him to move out. I kept after him, though, and now he is a delight to ride, swinging along freely in all gaits from the lightest of aids. This type of horse needs to be ridden at a very forward rising trot until it truly understands that it must work.

The opposite side of the coin is the nervous horse that shoots off at a great rate of speed the moment it feels your leg, usually with quick short steps. This type of horse needs to accept the pressure of your leg just as much as the first type. Do not make the mistake of taking your leg away to calm the horse; what happens when you put the leg back on? The horse flies away again. A soft, clinging leg that refuses to go away must be kept on the horse until it understands the leg will not go away no matter how fast it runs or plunges. It will gradually learn to slow down.

These are the two extremes, but all horses fall into some degree of sluggishness or speed. Both are problems that have to be resolved. The first type needs to go on long straight lines and on big circles, and be relentlessly pushed forward. The second type is easier to keep on a circle and you can use the circle to calm it down. Once the horse discovers that running gets it nowhere and that your leg will not disappear, it will tend to slow itself down. You are then in a position to use your leg to urge it on, but this time it is your idea; you are in charge. That is one of the keys to good training—you should make the decisions, not the horse.

In the early days you have few options as to what exercises to use. You have the choice of straight lines and big circles, but you must be very correct in both these exercises so that the horse can develop the necessary balance and suppleness for the future. If things are wrong at the beginning, you will never make any progress towards collection and agility.

The horse must first go forward. Once that lesson is successful, you must make the horse go straight, which is much easier said than done. The most difficult thing in all riding is to make the horse straight.

The power of the horse is developed in the hindlegs and transmitted through the spine to the forehand. Unless the forehand and hindquarters are correctly aligned, you lose some of the power from behind; it is wasted. In order to be efficient, the power plant has to remain squarely behind the mass to propel it forward. A horse has four legs, two sides and two ends; your job is to align each part and to help the horse use its natural strength to shift its weight in balance. As stated before, the rider's weight dramatically changes the horse's natural balance so the horse must be assisted in finding a new balance. The exercises we use are designed to rebalance and strengthen the horse systematically.

A horse is built like a wedge: it is narrower in the shoulders than in the hips. To put it straight on a straight line, you must always keep this fact in mind. When you ride down the side of the school or arena, the horse's natural tendency is to lean with its shoulders to the security of the wall; it goes crooked, with the shoulders slightly out and the hindquarter in. You must use the outside rein to

The horse is built like a wedge.

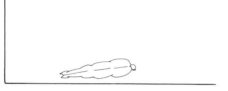

As the horse is narrower in front, the horse's natural tendency is to move down the track with the forehand leaning toward the wall. Sometimes this appears as if the hindquarters are falling in but it is usually not the case.

place the shoulders in the middle of the track and the inside rein to guide the nose a fraction to the inside, without placing weight on the inside shoulder. As the horse approaches the end of the long side and sees that it must turn the corner, nine times out of ten it will drop its weight to the inside in anticipation of the turn and fall to the inside. If the rider also anticipates by leaning into the turn, it makes matters worse. Your inside leg needs to push the weight to the outside before the turn, and with some horses you may even have to resort to using the whip on the shoulder in the early stages. Do not try to catch the weight

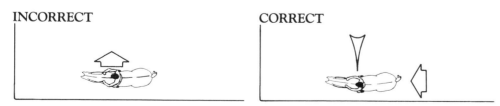

As you approach the corner, the horse will tend to fall in as it anticipates the turn. When you just pull the inside rein, this enables the horse to fall in on the inside shoulder or "pop" the outside shoulder. Instead, before the corner use a strong inside leg to push the horse through the turn and maintain the contact on the outside rein to keep the shoulders from falling in.

on the inside rein; if you do this, you teach the horse that you will support its weight on the inside. It will happily let you carry it around the turn; it is learning to avoid work. Further, the inside rein can be grossly misused and can create a crooked horse quicker than you can blink. The horse must turn the corner by pushing the mass from behind, not by falling on the forehand in the turn. In addition, you need to stay centered.

These same principles apply to making circles of any size. The horse must motor through from behind and not fall in or out, and you must not lean in, but must stay in the middle.

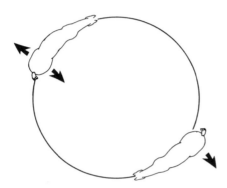

Bending on the circle. Often when you bend the horse's head to the circle, the hindquarters will drift to the outside. And the smaller the circle, the more the horse tries to avoid bending by letting the hindquarters drift. You must hold the hindquarters on the circle with your outside leg slightly behind the girth and keep the shoulders on the circle with your outside rein.

The circle is the most basic of all movements in dressage. All school figures are based on straight lines and circles which get progressively more demanding as training progresses. So it stands to reason that you must take extreme care in the first circles to ensure that they are always correct, so you can build towards future exercises. It sounds simple but a circle is ROUND: a circle does not have bulges, lumps, or bumps; it starts and finishes in the same place. *If the circle is not round, the value of the gymnastic is lost* because the horse avoids the difficulty.

On a circle the horse has to stretch the muscles on the outside of the body, give and bend the joints of the inside hind leg, and soften the muscles on the inside. A circle serves to stretch and bend the two sides of the horse. The horse must be able to balance its entire length without falling in or out of the curved line. It must bend from the inside leg pressing on the girth and send its weight into the outside rein, which will control the amount of bending in the body. Depending upon the size of the circle, the rider's outside leg will move back to hold the hindquarters on the curved line – the smaller the circle the further back the outside leg.

When you bring the horse's head to one side, it will usually move its hindquarters in the opposite direction to avoid having to bend. Your job is to teach it to bend and stretch so that the muscles will develop correctly. What you do

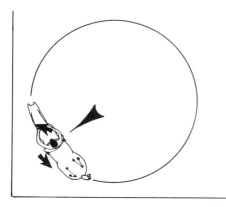

In the corner or on the circle maintain the horse's straightness. That is, keep the hindquarters aligned behind the forehand by using a supportive inside leg with the outside leg slightly behind the girth to keep the hindquarters from drifting out. Hold the outside rein close to the neck to prevent the shoulders from bulging outwards. If the hindquarters step up under the body, the horse can push through the corner or circle with no loss of balance.

on one side of the horse will always have a reaction on the other, and you must be prepared to deal with both sides.

In the beginning stages we are talking about limited amounts of bend, but you must be correct so that the horse will develop the correct suppleness.

Each horse will present different problems, but the well balanced horse should not have any difficulty in making a rounded circle. One direction will probably be easier than the other. A short coupled horse will have greater difficulty in bending than the average horse, and the long backed horse will be more inclined to become crooked, and wobble from side to side like a worm. Thoroughbreds that have been raced may be one-sided as they only ran one way on the track, and you will have to work at developing the right side. Horses that are locked in their shoulders have trouble in balancing on a circle, and horses with weak backs tend to go hollow and leave their hindquarters out behind them.

The circle is the universal exercise as long as it is correctly designed. But you do not want to bore your horse with endless circles, so mix up the exercises. Be as creative as you can and keep the work fresh each time you school. There is nothing worse than going round and round on the same circle for fifteen minutes. The more advanced the horse's training, the more options you have for patterns to run, but even at the beginning change constantly.

Ride down the side, make a circle, ride across the diagonal, ride a circle the other way; ride a circle in the middle of the arena (more difficult since you have no walls to help you). Turn down the center line and change the rein, turn across the middle and change the rein. Above all, make frequent transitions during all the figures—walk, halt, walk; walk, trot, walk, halt. Ride trot to halt through the walk at the start, then try for trot, halt, and trot again without the intermediate steps in walk. Each transition that you make downwards, through the use of your back and weight, makes the horse shift its weight from front to back. Transitions ridden only by using the reins keep the weight on the forehand. Each upwards transition that you make improves the thrust of the hindlegs. All of these transitions will lead to effective half halts later on.

At this stage you should be using a direct open rein for turning and making circles, supported by the outside rein to keep the shoulders in line. Your aids must be crystal clear and smooth so the horse can understand. Your legs, seatbones and back work in conjunction with the hands, but the golden rule should be "legs before hand." In other words, create some energy, then direct it. Don't confuse the horse by using the aids all at once; get it moving, position, and then balance it. The aid to go forward from the halt, for instance, will be to tighten your legs on the girth, then relax the arms and allow the horse to move forward. To halt from the walk, move your legs back a fraction, close them on the horse's sides, hold your back still for an instant, and tighten your arm muscles. In other words "leg-seat-hand," only they run together as "legseathand," with the time between each aid only a split second. If you use the hand first, the horse will put more weight onto the forehand and become heavy in front. By driving first with the legs, you create impulsion which you can then halt. *Any downward transition has to be ridden from back to front, and forward*, if the horse is to engage instead of falling on the forehand.

A transition ridden with the reins will be on the forehand and out of balance.

Drive the horse towards the transition. Don't think about stopping but think instead about shifting down to a gear with more power, not less.

Once you have basic control of your horse, all of these exercises can be worked on out in the open. In fact, you should be using undulating ground to help the horse find its balance; the horse was not designed by nature to go round and round in a flat ring. There is no better muscling exercise than to ride an active trot up a long slope and down again. The uphill work develops thrust and encourages the horse to stretch forward, while downhill work brings the hindlegs under the body (provided, of course, you don't let the horse just fall downhill on the forehand but support it with the rein and keep your legs on).

As the horse develops more balance, it is good to let it canter for short distances outside on the flat. I find that the confines of a school can be too demanding for some young horses in canter at first, unless the horse is exceptionally well balanced. Outside, let the horse develop the canter on a straight line; it does not

A young horse learning to keep its balance downhill. It needs to bend the joints of the hindquarters more. Be patient and keep riding forward without rushing.

Use uphill work to develop thrust from behind. This horse is actively stretching forward and down.

particularly matter which lead it picks up. If you are lucky enough to have a friend to ride out with, have the other horse canter off and join it.

To teach the horse to pick up the correct canter lead in the school, the best place to ask is going into a corner at the end of a long side. Use the inside leg at the girth to prevent the horse from falling to the inside, and place the outside leg behind the girth to signal the outside hind to step under the body for the depart. Since the canter will begin from the outside hind, you need to have the horse in good balance with your outside rein against the shoulder and your inside rein as light as possible. Take your outside rein slightly upwards and use the same command you used when the horse was on the lunge, "Can-ter!", as you give the leg aid. If the horse does not respond with the canter, try again at the end of the next long side. If the horse does canter, let it canter through the short

I believe the horse finds a better balance more quickly if you ask for the canter depart holding the outside rein high. The horse then cannot run onto the forehand.

Although the canter is not nearly active enough yet, the horse is relaxed and not leaning on the reins for support.

end of the school and let it come back to trot somewhere on the side. Be effusive with your praise. *And go back and do it again right away*, at least once.

Do some more trot work, then try the other lead using the same technique. If you succeed in obtaining both leads a couple of times, dismount, give your horse a reward and put it away for the day.

Some horses have great difficulty with one lead or the other, and with these you must try several different methods until you discover one that works. Details for this are included in the chapter on canter.

If the horse takes the incorrect lead during this work, allow it to canter for some strides before returning to the trot. "But it is disobedient," you say, but perhaps you asked when the horse was not properly placed, or at the wrong moment. The crucial point is that the horse cantered when asked. If you punish it, you build up resentment and confusion. Later you are going to want the horse to take the "wrong" lead in counter-canter; if you have punished it for cantering on the incorrect lead, it will be thoroughly confused at this point. I have ridden horses that have been punished for the wrong lead, and it took a great deal of tact and patience to persuade them I did want them to counter-canter. *Whatever you teach at the beginning of training must be a building block for the future.* Remember that horses are like elephants, they never forget. That can come back to haunt you in later exercises.

The beginning exercises

Exercise One: At the halt take up the contact and wait until the horse gives the jaw. Walk forward, energetically using your legs to encourage the horse to swing its barrel from side to side. Close your legs, stop your body movement for a second, push the horse into your hands and halt. Repeat all around the school. Relax the reins and let the horse stretch down and walk freely.

Exercise One. *The halt, with the horse prepared to move on. The horse is square but not engaged. Later in training, the horse must halt with the hindquarters under the body.*

Exercise One *continued. Relax the rein and let the horse stretch forward and out but still stay active.*

Exercise Two: Ride forward in walk and move up into trot. Use your legs close to the girth; if necessary, give a good sharp kick, and lighten your hand. Ride forward in rising trot, use the whip to reinforce the leg if necessary. Ride around the school, across the diagonals, changing direction frequently. Ride transitions between trot and walk, and trot again, and throw in the occasional halt.

Not enough energy here; the hindquarters are not active.

More active here. Although the horse is still hollow, it will soon relax if ridden forward. Don't try to force the horse into a preconceived shape; ride forward and the horse will come onto the bit.

Exercise Three: Ask the horse to make a 20-meter circle at the ends of the arena, keep the rhythm and energy. Most horses, once you leave the security of the perimeter of the school tend to wobble; keep the momentum. Circle at one end, cross the diagonal, and circle at the other end. Use a direct rein on the inside supported by the outside rein on the shoulder. Keep the inside leg at the girth, and the outside leg slightly behind the girth to keep the hindquarters from falling out of the circle.

Exercise Four: Ride a circle in trot to the left, go down the track, then ride a circle in the middle, being careful to make the circle rounded and fat. Don't let the horse fall in and squash the circle. Ride down the track and ride a circle at the far end. Change the rein and ride three circles to the right, one at the end, one in the middle and one at the far end. Make a transition to halt. Loosen the reins and let the horse relax in walk.

Exercise Five: When the horse can manage the three large circles, you can begin to ask for half-circles that are smaller in diameter. Ride down the school and make a half-circle to the center line and return to the track straight. You can also turn across the center line and change the rein. Turn down the center line and change the rein. Later, change the rein through the circle. The number of ways you can change direction are not limited to simply going across the diagonal, and the good trainer will never train a horse to a routine but will be inventive, coming up with new exercises every day so the horse stays fresh and interested. How often do you hear people say that dressage is boring? It is only boring if you do it by rote.

Exercise Six: The serpentine requires the horse to change direction and bend constantly, and is invaluable in reschooling the one-sided horse. A serpentine of two loops is actually a figure eight the length of a small arena; a serpentine of three loops is a series of 20-meter half-circles; a serpentine of five or six loops is better left until the horse develops more suppleness. A serpentine with an even number of loops will result in a change of rein, while a serpentine with an uneven number of will finish in the same direction it beings—a useful thing to remember when you design freestyle rides.

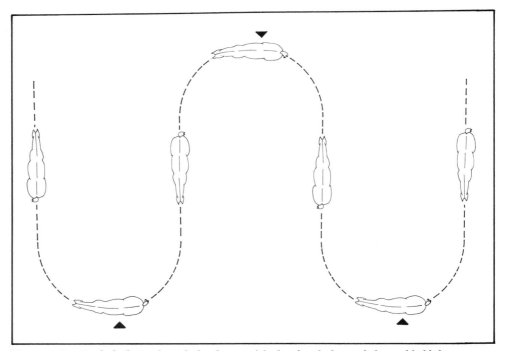

Exercise Six. *Push the horse through the change of the bend with the inside leg and hold the hindquarters on the line with the outside leg. Think about making the serpentine "fat" by pushing towards the outside; don't let the horse drop to the inside on the turns.*

During all of these exercises, ride frequent transitions and don't forget to include breaks when the horse is allowed to stretch out on a long rein. Keep it relaxed; don't hammer at the exercises.

For the first month or so it is best to keep the canter work simple. Just ride a circle at the end of the school until you can get the horse to pick up each lead reliably. The horse with poor balance in the canter will need to make lots and lots of transitions. If you stay in canter a long time, it will only become more and more unbalanced. Ask for a few strides of canter, return to trot, and pick up the canter again immediately. The horse has to bring the hindquarters under for the depart and the canter will eventually become lighter in front. Take your time, and above all, don't try to keep the horse in too short a canter stride at the beginning; let it go forward even if it feels as if you are flying. *Forward first.*

The better balance you develop in walk and trot, the better the canter will become, but the canter always develops last.

Exercise Seven: From the very beginning you must be thinking about getting your horse to lengthen and shorten its body and stride. This work can begin in the walk.

Put the horse into an energetic walk, and press both legs at the girth to push the horse up to your hand. Keep your body stretched and try to draw the horse up together under your seat. Walk a few steps in a short stride, then drop your hand forward and elongate your arm, allowing the horse to drop its head and neck forward. Increase the swing of the horse's back by using alternate legs to encourage it to step out and take longer strides. Then increase the leg pressure, hold with the hands and push the horse towards its head and shorten it. Repeat several times until you can feel the horse stretching forward and lengthening its stride when you reach out your arm. Short walk, long walk, short walk, long walk, short walk, halt. Loosen the reins and pat the horse. You should refine this skill until you can just close the leg and have the horse shorten itself up, and you can drop your hand forward and have the horse reach out and swing its back freely.

You can develop the same exercise in trot. On a circle, sit to the trot and draw the horse together by increasing the leg pressure while resisting gently with the hands. Then drop your hand a fraction forward and begin rising, pushing the horse forward with your legs. Sit again and use your leg to push the horse together; push to lengthen and push again to shorten—the same action gets the two results, like the man who blows on his soup to cool it and blows on his fingers to warm them.

Exercise Eight: Ride a small circle at the beginning of the long side, then ask the horse to lengthen its stride down the track, just as you have taught it on the lunge line, then ride another small circle at the end to shorten it. As you change from the small circle, straighten the horse with the outside rein and send it vigorously forward. Allow your hands to go towards the head; don't let the reins slip through your fingers as you will only have to reel them in again. Just stretch your arm forward, and then when you sit, bring your hands back towards your body. Don't try and lengthen the entire long side at first; let the horse give you a few longer steps, then compress it and ride a small circle. If you ask for too many steps at once, the horse will probably fall onto the forehand and run. Lengthen, then rebalance by coming back; in this way you will keep the hindquarters under the mass where it can propel it correctly.

Out in the country find a gentle slope and ride the horse uphill in a long stride and compress it downhill. Keep the rhythm, but allow the horse to stretch its *entire body and neck*, and then *push it from behind* to compress it again. This is the way to a proper lengthening and eventually extensions. Above all, don't let the horse hurry and run. A correct extension looks like the slow motion run of the Six Million Dollar Man—a long slow stride that hovers above the ground.

◇ 5 ◇

ACTIVATING
THE HINDQUARTERS

Once your horse is moving freely forward on the lunge, in a good rhythm in trot and canter, has been introduced to the work in hand, and can carry itself in balance under the rider on straight lines and large circles, it is time to begin work on suppleness and strength. The young horse should be at this stage after six to eight weeks of training, depending on the age of the horse. Most horses are not developed enough for formal training until they are four. While you can back them and ride them at three, it is best to leave serious training until their fourth year, when their bones have had a chance to develop.

For the older horse, or the horse that is undergoing rehabilitation, the early stages can be compressed into three or four weeks. If you have serious physical defects to overcome, it may take longer; it depends on the age and physical condition of the horse when you start work, and, of course, on the temperament.

All dressage training is aimed towards improving the horse's natural athletic ability. We do not teach the horse the lateral work simply to enter the different levels of competition. We teach the lateral work to improve the horse's ability to handle its body and to develop its muscles in a logical, progressive sequence. One exercise leads to the next and it is important to understand just what each entails and what it can do for the horse. And it is absolutely essential to understand that there are no short cuts without courting disaster in one form or another. Any gymnastic program takes time if it is to be effective in the long run. Muscles do not develop overnight, and if you force the horse into exercises without building the necessary muscles, you will end up with an unhappy, confused horse that hurts.

On the other hand, once you begin your program of muscle development, each horse will progress at a different rate, one that is individual to each animal. Some horses will have a natural aptitude for certain exercises and learn them early on. The training program has general guidelines but does not consist of absolute, rigid rules. There is more than one road to Rome.

The work in hand has introduced the idea of lateral work into the horse's mind. It knows it has to cross its legs over and bend its joints; now you need to transfer that idea over to mounted work.

I find the easiest way to teach a new exercise is to teach it in walk. The horse moves each leg separately and has time to displace its weight. Provided the horse is walking with energy and you keep it going forward, this is the best way to proceed. There is plenty of time later on to add impulsion once the horse has understood the lesson. Once it can maneuver in walk, you can repeat the lesson in trot and then in canter with less confusion.

Exercise One: Leg-Yielding.

Leg-yielding is not a classical exercise, but a means to an end with that end being the lateral work: shoulder-in, haunches in and out, and half pass. Leg-yielding is merely a stage, and should be discarded as soon as the horse is able to perform the lateral movements properly.

Since leg-yielding has been included in dressage tests in the United States, some confusion has arisen on both how it should be ridden and how it should be judged. The important thing is that the horse should move away from your leg promptly, without losing rhythm, without shortening its strides, and without losing its balance. The amount of bend is relatively unimportant. In fact, since you eventually want the horse to be able to bend in the direction it is moving in the half pass, I believe that the less bend it has in leg-yielding the better. You will not have to reeducate the horse later to perform the half pass. The horse will more than likely assume a slight bend towards the leg you are using, away from the direction of the movement, but it is still acceptable if it stays straight in its body.

The introduction to teaching the horse to move from your leg is teaching the horse the turn on the forehand. Halt near the wall facing left, for example, and

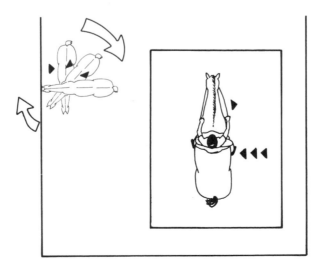

The turn on the forehand, performed from a halt. The right hand guides the head to the right with light pressure. The right leg is behind the girth, pushing the hindquarters to left, step by step: press, relax, press again. Don't just clamp the leg on and push hard or the horse may well resist and lean on your leg. The left rein prevents the neck from overbending, while the left leg stays passive but still in contact.

move your right leg back behind the girth. Step by step, push the horse's hind-quarter to the left. Your right rein indicates to the horse that its head should come to the right and the left rein prevents too much bend in the neck. Take it one step at a time and pat the horse as soon as it takes even one step around.

In the beginning, the horse will try to swing its front to the right and turn around its middle. It is your job to keep the front end in one place and move the back end around it. The idea here is that the horse steps away from your leg and displaces the hindquarter. Once you have been able to accomplish this to the left, start over and do the same exercise to the right.

As soon as the horse has learned to move from your leg, the turn on the forehand has served its purpose and you can forget about it!

Now you need to teach the horse to move from your leg while moving forward. Turn on the center line and ask it to move sideways back to the wall. Again,

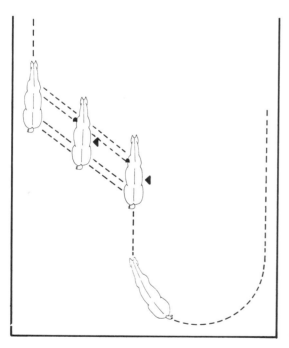

The leg-yield from the center line to the wall.

the horse will seek the security of the wall and this is probably the easiest way to teach the movement. The key to success is the timing of the leg aid. If you are asking the horse to move from the right leg, use your leg just behind the girth at the moment the left foreleg takes a step. This is because the next leg in se-quence will be the right hind and you want to push it sideways as it comes off the ground. If you ask the horse to move a leg that is still in support, it cannot obey and will naturally resist. As you use the leg to create movement, you must be ready to catch the energy in your left hand; otherwise the horse will just fall

The aids must be coordinated—soft and quick. If you just put your leg on and hold it there, the horse will hollow and resist.

With a soft, relaxed aid, the horse accepts the leg and moves sideways without resistance. The rider should look in the direction of the movement.

sideways out of balance. The leg and hand must work together—whatever the leg creates, the hand must regulate and balance.

If the horse speeds up when you use your leg, perhaps you are using too strong an aid. Just because you are doing a new exercise you do not have to increase the strength of your aid. If the horse is "on the aids," it will listen to a light touch, and if it doesn't, use your whip to call it to attention.

Dressage work requires concentration from horse and rider. When you are working, you are working, and the horse must understand this. Work for short, intense periods, then take time out when the horse can relax and gaze around. But *if you ask the horse to do something—enforce it.*

Leg-yielding can also be ridden down the track with the horse's head to the wall and its hindquarters inside the track. Or it can be ridden with the horse's head and shoulders off the track and the hindquarters swinging out—a preliminary form of shoulder-in. Later you can go from the track to the center, and combine this with stretching forward on the center line.

This work is preparation for the lateral exercises and should be used for as short a time as possible. Each horse will be different. Once the horse is confident in the walk, move on to the trot and repeat all the variations until the horse can easily move to either side without losing rhythm, balance or impulsion.

 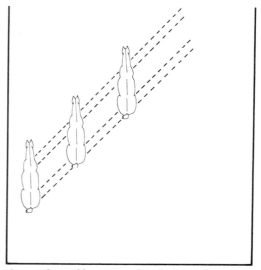

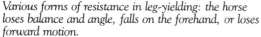

Various forms of resistance in leg-yielding: the horse loses balance and angle, falls on the forehand, or loses forward motion.

Correct leg-yielding. Note that the horse shows very little bend.

Exercise Two: Shoulder-in.

Shoulder-in is the most important exercise you teach your horse. It is the main road to suppleness, engagement and correct muscle development—*provided it is correctly taught and ridden.* The French master de la Guériniere, who invented the movement, said "It is the first and last lesson you must teach a horse." Nuno Oliveira said "shoulder-in is the aspirin of equitation, provided it is correct; otherwise it is poison." Shoulder-in can be used to straighten a horse, to balance a horse, to develop muscle, and to bring the horse into a state of collection. It can be used at any time during the horse's training as a correction for disobedience or resistance.

Classical shoulder-in is ridden in collection, but in the early stages you can sacrifice some of the collection until the horse is strong enough to carry itself properly.

As an intermediate step between leg-yielding and shoulder-in, you can use the spiral in and out on the circle. Ride your horse on a large circle to the left, then gradually reduce the size of the circle by pushing the hindquarters towards the center with your right leg behind the girth. At the same time take both hands to the left; your right rein will come against the neck and your left hand will lead the horse inwards. To prevent the horse from merely falling into the circle, your left leg must stay at the girth and the horse must maintain a bend around this inside leg. The horse should soften to the inside as you reach the smaller circle. After one or two revolutions on the small circle of approximately 10 meters, enlarge the circle again by using light touches of your left leg. *The horse should*

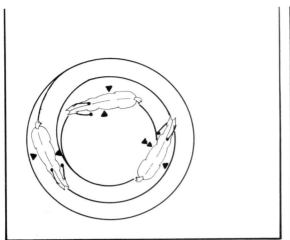

The spiral, with the same bend both in and out, is useful as a beginning to the shoulder-in.

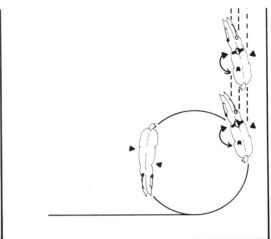

Shoulder-in can be taught from a small circle. Here, the rider's left leg aid should be timed to drive the horse's left hind under the body. The rider's right leg stays behind the girth to prevent the hindquarters from falling out with the horse avoiding the necessary bend.

stay in the same bend as you push it outwards. The difference between this exercise and leg-yielding is that the horse remains bent to the inside as it moves from one leg inwards and as it moves from the other leg outwards.

This exercise can be worked in walk and then in trot, and should be followed by some energetic forward work in rising trot — *never forget to go forward after teaching a new skill*.

Shoulder-in can be taught from a small circle ridden at the beginning of the long side. To the left, ride the short end of the arena in an energetic and rhythmic walk, with the horse bent around your left leg. Lead the horse onto a small circle with your left hand, while the right hand stays close to the shoulder to keep the horse aligned on the circle and to prevent the neck from overbending or the right shoulder from popping out. Your right leg stays slightly behind the girth to hold the hindquarters on the circle. All your aids are now correctly placed for the shoulder-in; you do not have to change the position of your hands or legs.

As you reach the wall at the end of the circle, use your left leg as if you wanted to push the horse out on the circle as you did in the spiral. Bring the hands to the inside, almost as if you were going to begin another circle. The horse's shoulders, *both of them*, come to the inside of the track while you push the horse towards your right rein. Turn your shoulders to the inside so they remain parallel to the horse's, and squeeze your right rein.

The most common faults in shoulder-in are caused by the rider trying to pull the head and neck in with the inside rein. This causes the horse to fall onto the inside shoulder and it nearly always falls forward into the school, instead of stay-

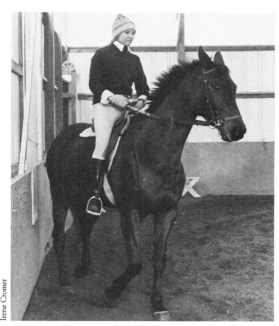

Incorrect. This is neither a leg-yield or a shoulder-in. The horse is not accepting the aids and is hollow.

Too much emphasis on the head and neck, a common fault that accomplishes nothing. The exercise must come from the legs first; it will not succeed by just using the reins.

Better angle, with better impulsion and balance.

ing on the track. The weight must remain on the horse's *inside hind leg* if the horse is to benefit from this exercise correctly. Remember the shoulders must come in, not just the head and neck. Bring the outside shoulder in with the outside rein.

Another mistake is to overbend the neck without shifting the shoulders at all. The neck should remain relatively straight; the degree of bending will depend upon the length of the neck and the degree of suppleness of the horse. In the early stages, ask for just a small bend.

Some riders try to push the shoulders sideways with the inside rein used indirectly, but all this accomplishes is to make the horse crooked and unbalanced so it loses rhythm and twists its head.

You need to ride the horse from your left (inside) leg towards the outside hand. Your leg must be used in time with the stepping of the horse's left hind as it leaves the ground in order to push it under the body. Your leg should then be relaxed until the horse's leg is ready to take the next step. If you just keep pushing, the horse will likely lean on your leg and not carry itself. Your right hand needs to catch the energy created by the left leg. The action of the hand is subtle. Imagine that you are holding hands with someone and you want to give a friendly squeeze; that is the feeling you need. Your hand does not have to move at all, just use your fingers briefly and relax them again. At each step use your left leg to push the horse sideways and under, and squeeze your right rein. Left leg—right rein— left leg—right rein; in this way you keep the horse in good rhythm but you do not block its movement.

Your left (inside) hand will have little to do; it stays passive. Your right (outside) leg remains behind the girth to hold the hindquarters on the track, to urge them forward, and to prevent them from falling out. If the horse does not bend the spine, the exercise performed is jut a leg-yield with the head inside. Shoulder-in requires a bend.

Be content with a few steps at first. As soon as the horse steps nicely under and sideways, allow it to stretch its neck and pat it. Repeat the exercise down the long side, and be content with a few steps at a time.

If you run into a lot of resistance—the horse stiffens, or throws its head up, or runs through your hands when you use the leg—put the horse back onto the small circle and regroup until you have it balanced. Then try again. Don't try and force the horse; don't use strength to make the horse do the exercise. The horse must learn to do the exercise by itself—your job is to place the horse into the correct balance and allow it to perform. If you have to hold it by force, your training is drastically at fault. Make sure your aids are correct and given at the exact moment they will be effective; don't confuse the horse.

After a few minutes spent on teaching the shoulder-in, move the horse forward to trot to reestablish forward momentum. Remember, don't drill the horse too long.

As you progress with this exercise, the horse will come to understand what you want and you can ask for longer periods of shoulder-in. If you run into resistance, ride a small circle and restart every time. After a week or so, you should be able to ride a small circle at the beginning of the school, go halfway down the track in shoulder-in, ride another small circle and complete the side in shoulder-in. If you are both consistent and persistent, the horse should catch on easily. As soon as it can work in the shoulder-in at the walk without losing rhythm and without resistance on both sides, you can move on and perform the movement in trot.

Each horse is different; some learn quickly while others seem to have great blocks to understanding. You have to be persistent and, above all, patient. If you keep repeating the same exercise, using the correct aids time after time, the horse will eventually catch on. Sometimes I must confess it seems as if you are getting nowhere day after day, but you have to have faith in the system and keep on. When you teach a new movement, keep at it day after day. If the horse has trouble at first, it will likely catch on if you repeat daily. If you only try once a week, you run the risk of starting all over at square one each time. A horse learns by daily repetition; once it has understood, however, use the exercise only when needed.

When the horse can execute a balanced shoulder-in on both sides, in walk and trot without losing balance or rhythm, you can use the exercise in many ways to improve the horse's engagement, strength and suppleness:

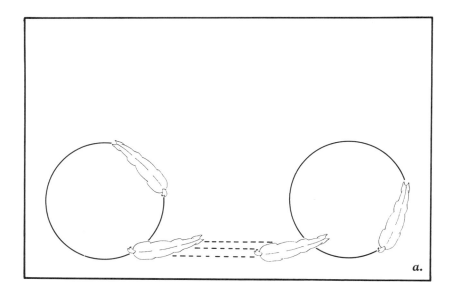

a. Small circle to shoulder-in to small circle.

b. Shoulder-in left on the long side, turn across the middle, turn right at the wall, and shoulder-in right.

c. Shoulder-in down the side making frequent transitions in and out of halt.

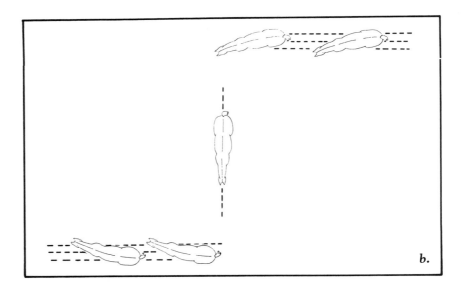

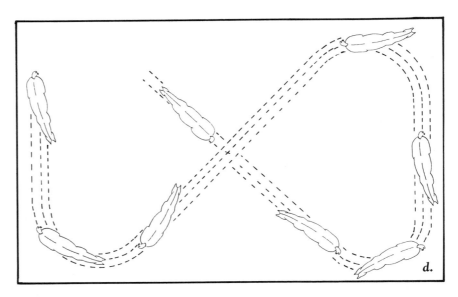

d. Shoulder-in on the short side, shoulder-in across the diagonal, reverse shoulder-in through the other short side and down the track, back across the diagonal. At X, straighten and extend the gait.

e. Shoulder-in on a large circle. Later, decrease the size of the circle by spiralling in and out.

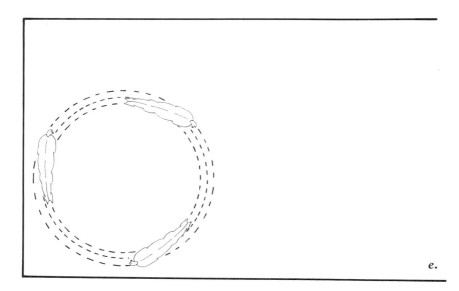

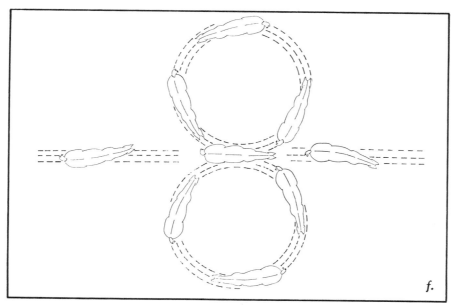

f. Shoulder-in down the center, continue in shoulder-in on a 10-meter circle at X, straighten, change the bend, then perform a 10-meter circle the opposite way, and shoulder-in again.

The patterns are limited only by your ingenuity; don't get stuck in the rut of doing only the exercises required in tests.

The shoulder-in prepares the foundation for all advanced work.

The end result. A balanced shoulder-in with impulsion and on three tracks: inside fore, diagonal outside fore and inside hind leg, and outside hind.

Exercise Three: The rein back.

The rein back is an excellent exercise to put the horse squarely onto its haunches, *provided the rein back is correctly performed and not overused.*

The rein back can be taught from the ground during the work in hand. You stand slightly in front of the horse and urge it to step backwards with your hand on the rein. For the horse that resists, you tap with the whip on the chest at the same time.

To perform a rein back when mounted, halt the horse on the track and keep the horse "on the aids" between your legs and your hands. You initiate some energy

The rein back. Alternate pressure of leg and hand controls the steps backwards: leg and hand on one side, followed by leg and hand on the other side.

with your legs and, for once in riding dressage, you incline your upper body slightly forward to push the horse's weight to the rear. As you use your legs, the horse will in all probability try to step forward as it has been taught. Stop the forward motion with your hand and take a slight backwards pull on one rein, then the other. If you try to force the horse back with both reins, it will probably throw its head up, hollow its back, and resist. If you use the leg and hand on one side to influence one hindleg, and then relax the aid and use the other hand and leg, the horse can accept the idea of stepping alternate legs backwards. Reward profusely at the slightest hint of backward motion and press the horse forward again with loose reins. Be content with one or two steps at first.

Make certain the horse stays straight; most horses will slide their rear end to one side or the other to avoid bending the joints of the hindleg. Correct any sideways deviation with the rein on the same side held out in opposition to the quarters. The key to the successful rein back is to use light aids that coordinate hand and leg on one side, and relax as soon as the horse begins each step. There is absolutely no need to pull; in fact, *if you pull, you will create resistance.* You want fluid, round steps backwards in a clear two-time rhythm.

A horse that reins back easily can always be put onto its quarters at any time.

Exercise Four: The haunches-in (travers).

Thus far the horse has been asked to work laterally when bent away from the direction of the movement. The next step on the ladder is to teach it to bend in the direction of the movement and use its joints even more. For some horses

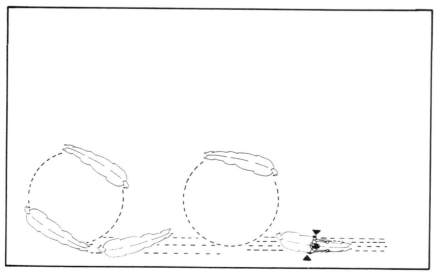

To teach the haunches-in, begin by riding a circle and then a few steps of shoulder-in. Ride another circle and, as you reach the track, prevent the haunches from reaching the track. The bend and position of the rider's hands and legs do not change. Only the emphasis of the leg aids change, as the right leg behind the girth holds the hindquarter to the inside.

this can be confusing. While they may have had little trouble learning the shoulder-in, they might find the **haunches-in** more difficult: short-backed horses in particular may have difficulty.

Begin with an exercise the horse knows well, a small circle to the left followed by shoulder-in and another small circle at the halfway point of the long side. *The positioning of your aids* — the left leg on the girth, right leg behind, left hand leading, right hand close to the shoulder — *does not change.* What does change is the emphasis. Your aim is to keep the horse's hindquarters from going all the way back to the track while allowing the shoulders to reach the track. *The horse remains bent around your inside leg* and you must remember to use it as well as the outside one.

Put your weight on your left seat bone and touch the horse with the right leg to push the right hind under the body. The horse should keep its head and neck looking straight down the track while the hindquarter curls around your left leg. Give and take on the inside (left) rein and keep your shoulders square to the track, parallel to the horse's shoulders.

The correct positioning for travers (haunches-in). The horse bends around the inside leg of the rider.

At first the horse will only be able to give you a slight bend to the inside and you must be content with just a little. As you progress with this exercise and the horse learns to bend the joints of the hindlegs, it will be able to show more angle. Be content with a little bend and a few steps at a time; then go forward onto another small circle.

You can also alternate this new exercise with the shoulder-in. Ride a small circle, then shoulder-in halfway down the long side, ride another small circle, and then ask for haunches-in. The shoulder-in frees up the shoulders and the haunches-in bends the hindquarters. In shoulder-in left, the horse brings the left hind over in front of the right; in haunches-in, the horse brings the right hind over in front of the left hind.

Exercise Five: The haunches-out (renvers).

Essentially this exercise is identical to the travers except that the horse moves along the track with the shoulders inside the school and the haunches on the track, bent in the direction of the movement. It serves to develop suppleness and the bending of the hindquarter.

Although the horse is actually too far off the rail, it is correctly bent for the haunches out.

Exercise Six: The Half Pass.

The half pass dramatically increases the horse's ability to bend the joints of the hindlegs. The horse moves on two parallel tracks, flexed slightly in the direction of the movement, but with a straight spine. This develops mobility in the hindquarters. When combined with the previous exercises, the half pass enables the horse to engage the hindquarters and collect its forces.

In shoulder-in, the inside hind leg propels the mass; in half pass, the outside hind has to step under and provide the thrust. After performing a half pass, you can take advantage of the increased engagement of the hind leg by straightening the horse and using the increased thrust of the hindquarters to send the horse energetically forward.

The easiest way to teach half pass is by making a half circle to the center line, and then riding half pass back towards the wall. On the half circle the horse is already bent to the inside, and you can send it back towards the wall without changing the bend. At first the horse may only manage to give you one or two steps before it loses the bend; when that happens, you should ride straight forward and begin again. Teach the exercise in walk until you can maintain the bend, then move on to trot.

Ride in shoulder-in down the wall and continue the shoulder-in to the center line. Ride one or two steps of shoulder-in up the center line and ask for half pass. The bend and the placement of the aids does not change; only the emphasis of the aids changes. In left shoulder-in, the left leg is at the girth, the right leg behind, while the left rein stays elastic and the right rein controls the shoulder. As you reach the center line, gently shift your weight to the left seatbone and use the right leg to push the right hind to the left, in front of the left hind. Again, pay special attention to the timing: use your leg as the diagonal foreleg is in the air. Your inside leg maintains the bend and impulsion.

The necessary suppleness and balance for all the lateral work develops gradually. You must be sure to maintain good impulsion throughout each new exercise. The most common fault in all lateral work is that the rider tries to go sideways too much all at once and the horse "sucks back," shortening its strides to avoid the difficulty. When this happens, the aids should not get stronger; don't try to force the horse with the rein. Send it with your legs and relax between each application of the leg. Energetic, straight, forward work must be included each time the horse falters. You must have a metronome in your head going "tick-tick-tick." Remember, the first collective mark on a dressage test is for the paces: *"Regularity and freedom."* If the rhythm changes, you lose *regularity*, and if you constrict the horse you lose *freedom*. Without these two essentials, dressage is nonexistent and your training is counterproductive.

When the half pass is established you can combine the lateral work in numerous patterns:

a. Half circle, then half pass to the wall each way.

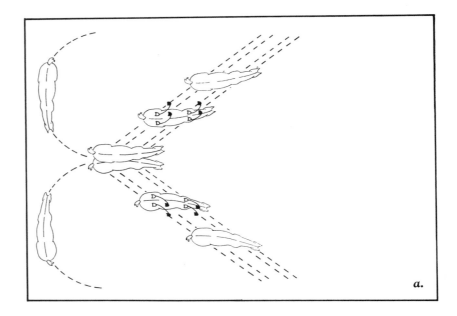

a.

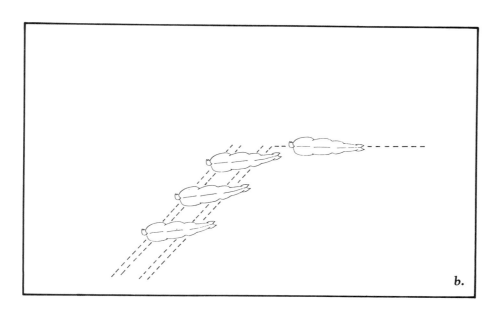

b. Half pass from the wall to the center and straight on.

c. Shoulder-in small circle, then half pass to the center.

d. Half pass to the center, one or two straight steps, change the bend, and half pass back to the wall. This is the first step in teaching counter change of hand.

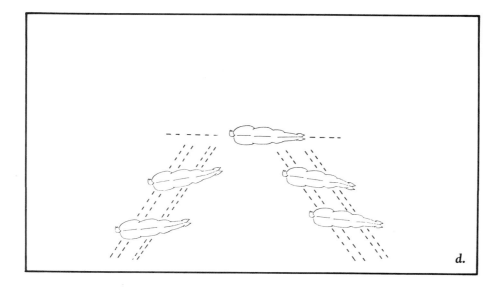

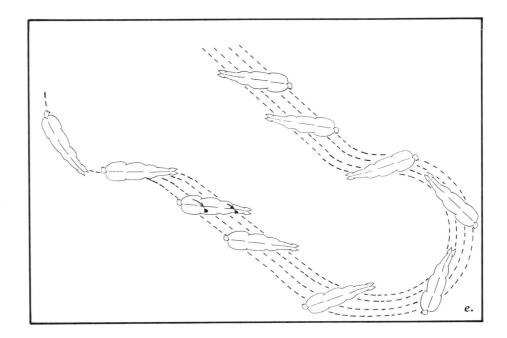

e. Turn down the center line, half pass to the wall. At the wall ride
   haunches out (renvers) and continue through the corner and back to
   the center line in renvers, then ride half pass back to the far wall.
   This is an exercise used by the old masters to "confirm the half pass."

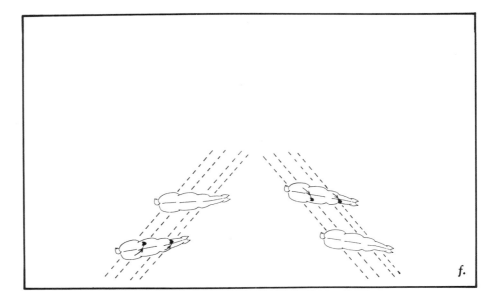

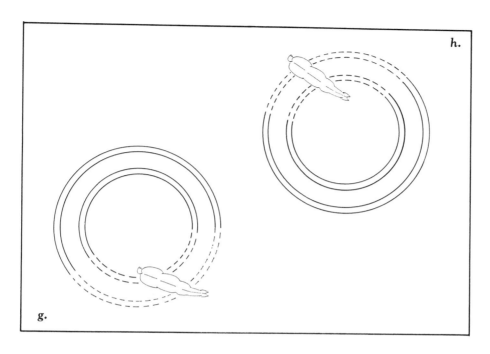

f. Ride counter change of hand: half pass to X from the wall, change the
   bend and half pass back to the wall. This is similar to *d*, but with
   fewer straight steps.

g. Ride a circle in half pass with the shoulders on the outside and the
   haunches inside the arc of the circle.

h. Ride a circle in half pass with the shoulders inside and the haunches
   outside.

The most common difficulties encountered in teaching the half pass exercises are losing the bend, leading with the hindquarters, and losing impulsion.

If the horse loses the bend, you can ride a few steps of shoulder-in to make
the horse move from your inside leg. The inside leg is more important in the
half pass than the outside leg because the inside leg has to keep the bend and
send the horse forward. Think of half pass as going "forward and over," not just
"over." The outside leg serves to indicate direction only.

Many people are so worried about getting into a half pass that they take the
outside leg back too soon and do not position the horse correctly. An excellent
rule to follow is "always start a half pass with one step of shoulder-in." Then you
have the horse bent to the inside leg, and you can be sure that the hindquarters
do not start off before the shoulders. Be careful not to use too much inside rein
against the inside shoulder as you will prevent the sideways movement of the
shoulders and block the inside hind leg. If you have a problem in moving the
shoulders to the side, the outside rein should press against the outside shoulder

A common mistake: the rider keeps the weight over the active leg although the horse is supposed to move in the opposite direction.

The horse is moving with the correct bend, head slightly tilted.

Correct positioning produces a supple half pass. It is not necessary to exaggerate the bend of the neck; in fact, this often causes a loss of impulsion.

to send it over. On the other hand, if you have trouble moving the hindquarters over, you can use the outside rein in opposition to the quarters by taking it away from the horse and back towards your hip.

I find the discussion of the reins of opposition, and direct and indirect influences of the reins extremely confusing. I like to think of the "inside" rein and the "outside" rein, and they can be used in a thousand different combinations for different effects. As you experience difficulties you will discover all manner of rein effects. I believe that the work in hand teaches rein effects very efficiently.

Only when the horse is confirmed in the ability to produce a balanced, rhythmical half pass in walk and trot should you attempt it in canter.

All the lateral exercises help activate the hindquarters, and as the horse progresses you will find it becomes lighter and more responsive each day. The length of time it will take to achieve good results will depend on each horse and your ability to communicate with it. The work outlined in this chapter, coupled with the work on extending the gaits and the work in canter may easily take nine months to a year or more to develop.

One step at a time should be your motto: "make haste slowly." Perfect one exercise before introducing the next, and give the horse time to understand. Each exercise the horse masters makes the next easier to assimilate. The horse learns by learning; its intelligence and concentration improves and once it trusts you, it becomes more receptive to new movements. It will understand the learning process if you reinforce the lessons with lots of praise and reward.

◊6◊

COMPETITION

As soon as your horse is doing the basic work, it is time to think about finding a competition to get the horse out and about. Any horse that can walk, trot, and canter in both directions and with some degree of balance and rhythm can compete at the Training Level.

Training Level is an introduction to competition and should be treated as such. It is a means to an end, that end being the higher levels.

Successful showing depends on being organized about all the details, not just riding the test. You are best off entering a schooling show, if possible, for the horse's first outing. Schooling shows are more relaxed, the judges are compassionate, and there is less red tape involved. And schooling shows are cheaper; don't blow your money on a recognized show if your horse is not prepared.

Get your entries in on time; even schooling shows are full. To ensure a place you must get your entry in, correctly filled out with all the necessary information: membership number, coggins test, and so on. Show secretaries are hard-working people and incomplete entries make their lives a misery.

Once you have entered, find out exactly how long it will take you to get to the show. That may sound stupid but you need to allow plenty of time to get to the showgrounds, with plenty of time to get your horse out of the trailer, tacked up and thoroughly warmed up before your riding time. On occasion I have arrived at a show five minutes before I was due in the ring, flung the tack on the horse and made it by the bell—but needless to say the performance lacked a lot. Allow for the unexpected: a flat tire, getting stuck in traffic, or other hazards.

It is nice to have some help at a show; perhaps you can persuade a friend to come along to groom for you? If the show is local, you do not have to find stabling but will have to work out of your trailer. If there are two of you, you will not have to leave your horse unattended in the trailer. Accidents can and will happen and I have seen too many horses injured when left alone. My rule is *never leave the horse without someone to keep an eye on it*, and *never leave a horse tied to a trailer unattended*. It takes just one incident to upset or spook the horse and it can whirl around and damage itself severely. You will then face wasted months while it recovers.

The horse should be squeaky clean, its mane smartly braided, and its tail pulled and banged. In dressage shows the tails should not be braided. The tack

Horse and tack must be clean and tidy. Be proud of your turnout; competition is a time to show off!

should be immaculate. Be proud of your turnout; you are presenting a "show" so make an impression from the start. Your own turnout should also be neat and tidy, with your hair under restraint in a hairnet. There is nothing worse than seeing a beautifully braided horse being ridden by someone whose hair flops up and down like the ears of an Irish setter. If your horse is well turned out, you need to match it.

At the first show, allow plenty of time for warm up. You will not be sure how your horse will react, so it's important to give yourself time to spare. As you continue showing, you will have a good idea of how long the horse needs before going in the ring. Some horses benefit from being lunged first for fifteen minutes or so. You can use the schooling shows to discover all this. I had one horse that, even once we were at Prix St. Georges level, would shy at the markers in the ring in his first test in the first show of the season. This was even after all the mileage he had at shows. So I always entered a preliminary test before the important one just to allow him to get that out of his system. That is what I mean by being prepared.

You should also note the time it takes you to braid and get ready at the barn before you leave. Some people braid the night before; as long as your horse does not rub the braids, you are safe. But, remember, braids always look tidier when freshly made.

Pack the night before, and put all your clean equipment in the truck or car. Make a list and check it several times. The rush getting ready to go frequently means you will forget something: a whip, a girth, or your gloves. Check each item off from your list as you load it.

I use an apron or wrap around skirt over my white breeches during the warm up phase because I find it impossible to keep spotless. I lunge and warm up with my coverups on.

After you have warmed up and it is nearly time to go (the nice thing about dressage shows is that they run on time *nearly always* but you should check to see they are keeping to the schedule), your kind helper can be put to work. The horse should be wiped over with a cloth to remove any last minute dust, the tail bandage taken off along with any protective wraps you have been using, hoof dressing put on, and the girth checked. Put on your coat, straighten up your stock or tie, make sure your hair is tucked in, put on your hat and gloves, and have your helper give your boots a last wipe.

Before you enter the ring, ride around the outside after the horse ahead of you has finished its test. You can usually start around the ring as soon as the

Warm up well and then get clean and tidy.

A workmanlike turn out. Horse and rider look ready for the job at hand.

rider before you has saluted. Let your horse look at the markers around the ring; let it stop in front of the judge and see the trailer or umbrella and the judge and scribe so that it is not surprised by them if they move about. Judges can seem scary to the inexperienced horse.

I had a young horse who at our first show never got past X; he decided that the judge and table were really dangerous. We struggled through the test, and I eventually got up near C after my ride. But that is precisely why you go to schooling shows—to school. The same horse jumped out of the ring at the next show, so I just jumped him back in and finished the test giggling throughout. At the third show, he won two classes, so the schooling paid off.

Usually someone will check your bit and spurs during the last few minutes. Be sure to get into the habit of looking for the steward for this purpose; don't make them chase you around.

Larry C. White

Allow your horse to look at all the
"demons" in the trailer and flower boxes.

When the whistle blows, or bell rings, line up on the center line and put your horse into a forward trot. Smile as you enter the ring. The judge's first impression can influence your first mark. Look as if you know what you are doing, and be relaxed, happy, and proud of your horse. Show off. That's what showing is about. Dressage has its roots in showing off; the traditions of dressage training come down from the courts of Europe where the kings and nobles rode horses to show off their skills. Exude confidence; it will carry you through. Many people look as if they are about to burst into tears in the show ring. You may feel like that, but don't show it; even if you are having problems, grit your teeth and grin.

Make your salute short and snappy. Don't lean off the side of your horse. Drop one hand—it doesn't matter which—but don't salute with the hand that holds your whip. You might hit your horse and ruin the entire movement. Nod your head, put your hand back on the rein, and move off at the trot. A man should remove his hat and drop it to his side, unless the hat has a harness. In that case, the salute is the same as for women. A military type salute is permissable only if you are in uniform. Judges see a great many variations on salutes, none of them correct. Don't wave at the judge like an old friend; make the salute smart.

The horse must remain immobile and square on all four feet. If it is nervous and fidgets around, get your salute over with and get moving forward. If the horse fiddles around, you have already blown that mark so get going and recoup the marks in the rest of the test.

Move straight forward and prepare your horse for the turn at C. The horse must have a regular rhythm and go forward easily, stretching to the bit. At Training Level, the horse must move freely forward. It should not need be constricted in any way. The requirement is that it accept the bit, not adopt a false position of the head and neck. When you change from rising to sitting trot, there should be absolutely no difference in the trot.

Circles at this level are all 20-meter (66 feet), the width of the arena. Remember, a circle is round, not oblong, not lopsided, doesn't have straight sides, and begins and ends at the same point. Right from the very beginning get your geometry correct. Precision of the figures cannot win a test alone, but precision coupled with correct movement can gain you valuable points.

After the dismal showing of American riders in the 1986 World Championships in Canada, someone said to me, "The Europeans won because they were so accurate." Nonsense—the Europeans won because they were not only brilliant, but also dead accurate in all transitions and figures. That is what made the difference. If the transition from extended canter to collected canter is called for at F, they ride it at F, they do not fudge it by coming back a marker early. If the movement starts at B, they are precisely at B. Right from the very start pay attention to your school figures; if you cheat on the figures, you cheat your horse out of the gymnastic benefit of the exercise. Accuracy is not all there is to dressage but it makes the difference between the champions and the merely good riders, *at any level*.

At Training Level, the transitions can be progressive, a few walk steps from the trot to the halt, a few walk steps from halt to trot. But if you can show a clean transition, you will get good marks. The directives are "transitions *may be* through walk," not that they have to be. Each movement should be ridden as the rider's body reaches the marker, not the horse's head, but in Training Level judges are more lenient. They prefer to see a smooth transition a little early than a bad one exactly at the marker. But when you move up to First Level, you can't get away with that any more. If you do a perfect transition at the exact mark, the judge cannot help but be impressed. After all, what is there to look at in Training Level except walk, trot and canter both ways of the ring, and the transitions between the gaits? Be sure to keep your eyes ahead and prepare for all the movements well in advance. As you turn up the center line at the end of the test, prepare the turn as you come to the end of the preceeding long side. This way you will be able to make a nice flowing turn onto the center line without overshooting or cutting in.

Ride straight down the centerline with just a bit more impulsion than before to help the straightness. Smile your biggest smile. Halt, make a smart salute, relax the reins, and walk out of the ring on a long rein.

If you have done your homework, a Training Level test should be smooth and flowing. The key to success is your schooling at home. Be confident and relaxed; if you are uptight, you can bet your horse will reflect the fact. Part of being confident is knowing the test you will ride upside down and back to front. Learn your test. If you feel you might have a lapse of memory your helper can read the test for you, but having a reader is no substitute for knowing what you are going to do. Training Level tests are so basic there is not much strain on your memory. If you are showing horses at several different levels, I think there is justification for using a reader. I find, however, that I make more errors in Training Level than any other because there is so little to do and I can't get used to merely riding down the long sides without making a move.

If you do use a reader, he or she should stand at E or B and read each movement as it is written on the test sheet, *no deviations*. The reader may read each movement only as it is written; repeating movements or talking to the rider is unauthorized and could eliminate you. If you don't hear your reader, don't shout "What? I can't hear!" If you do make an error, the judge will blow the whistle and set you straight again. Don't be rattled by this, just pick up, continue, and try to do even better to regain the two marks you receive for going off course.

After the test, cool your horse off and put it away unless you have another ride coming up right away.

Don't wear your horse out with constant warm up. Take whatever time you need before each test, but don't grind the horse into the ground. Two, or at the most three, tests per day are enough for the novice horse. When you take into consideration the travel, the excitement of being away from home, the warm up time, and then the actual riding of the test, the horse has a lot to do. Don't sour it at shows.

When you get to the show, it is time to show, not to school. Schooling takes place at home and showing is the end result.

As the horse becomes more advanced, you can move up to First Level, where you have to be more precise in transitions, show a lengthening of the gaits, and a leg-yielding. First Level is still very basic; horses should be ready for it in the first two or three months of training. If the schooling shows go well, you can enter the recognized shows.

For recognized shows, you need to have your horse registered with the various organizations if you are interested in awards or annual points. The horse needs to be registered with the American Horse Shows Association, the United States Dressage Federation, and your local dressage organization. There are so many award programs available that it becomes mindboggling to keep up with them. The AHSA is the national federation; if you have your eye on international competition in the future, you need to work through that body. But that concern is for the future.

When you get home, study your score sheet, and take it as an evaluation of your training program. I save all my score sheets and refer back to them time and again. The judge should have pinpointed the areas that need improvement and the areas that are going well. Study hard and adjust your training routines to take care of the weak points. Each successive test should show improvement; if not, you need to reconsider your program. Use the score sheet constructively; that is what it is for—it is the considered opinion of an expert on your horse's performance. Judges do care about the future of dressage; listen to them.

◇ 7 ◇
SPECIAL EXERCISES FOR PROBLEMS

The exercises in the previous chapters are progressive and will work for the majority of horses. However, all horses are not created equal; those that have been poorly trained or have conformation faults can use the extra help of specific exercises for specific problems. These can be used early on in training or retraining, but do not replace the classical exercises. Some are done from the ground or during lunge work, and some are mounted exercises.

Conformation Problems

The Short Back

The horse with a short back is usually strong but often will have difficulty bending. It also has a tendency to straddle its hindfeet outside the forefeet to avoid hitting itself. If the short back is coupled with a short neck, bending becomes even more difficult.

Exercise One: Unmounted flexion and stretching.

Stand beside the horse and hold the reins close to the bit. Vibrate the rein in your left hand and ask the horse to bring its head to the left. Wait until the horse softens the jaw, then return the head to a normal position. Repeat on the other side. Make sure the head remains at the level of the shoulder and do not let the horse twist its head so that the ears become unlevel. Often when you bring the head to one side, the horse will step away from you with the hindquarters to avoid bending. If this happens, place the horse beside the wall to prevent the evasion.

A short-backed horse with great power. The hind end must stay up under the body. Often this type is reluctant to engage because it doesn't want to step on itself.

You can teach the horse to bend away from you by pressure on the rein.

Exercise Two: Unmounted stretching.

For this exercise, the horse needs to be standing squarely on all four feet. Stand in front of the horse with one hand on either rein and wiggle the bit to gradually lower the horse's head towards the ground. Don't let the horse pull back towards its body; it must stretch *forward and down.*

Exercise Three: Spiral on the lunge.

When you lunge this type of horse, watch carefully to see that the hindquarters follow the forehand. Often the horse will go around the circle with the hind-quarters held to the outside. Try to push the horse as close to the wall as possible

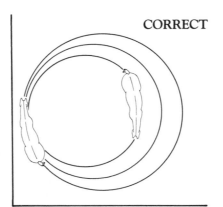

CORRECT

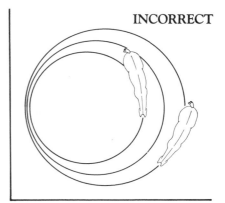

INCORRECT

Exercise Three. *The horse should ideally be able to keep the hindquarters on the circle as you decrease the size. A stiff horse will allow the hindquarters to remain on the outside. Take the time to develop the necessary suppleness.*

to encourage it to stay straight. Gradually decrease the circle by reeling in the lunge line. As soon as the horse shows crookedness, let it drift back out to the larger circle. Take all the time you need to get the horse onto a small circle with a correct bend.

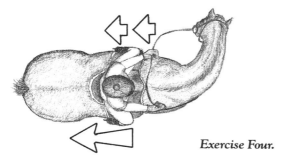

Exercise Four.

Exercise Four: Mounted stretching and flexing.

After you mount, repeat the first exercise by asking the horse to bend first to the left, then to the right. You need only take the head at a 90 degree angle to the body. Try to have the horse remain there with little or no contact for a few seconds. Don't force the head around with a heavy rein; a series of small tugs should indicate to the horse that it must move its head and neck. Ideally you want to place the horse, then relax the rein and have it stay there by itself. The difficulty in this exercise is that nine times out of ten the horse will move the hindquarters in the opposite direction. You need to keep contact on the opposite rein with the opposite leg well back to hold the hindquarters. When you first ask for the bend, do so inch by inch. Don't hurry; give the horse time to figure out what you want. The value of this exercise is not so much in the bending, but in the stretching of the opposing muscles. On some horses you will actually feel the muscles of the loin and stifle on the side opposite to the bend quiver.

The horse should not bring the head around this far; perpendicular to the neck and body is enough. But this does illustrate the flexibility of the neck.

Repeat this on both sides and you will quickly discover the horse's stiff side: the exercise will be much easier on one side than the other. This is a beneficial exercise at the start of your program for each day. How long should you use this particular exercise? It depends on each horse, but usually only for the first month; it is of limited value after that. In the beginning it serves both to help the horse stretch and to understand the bending action of the rein.

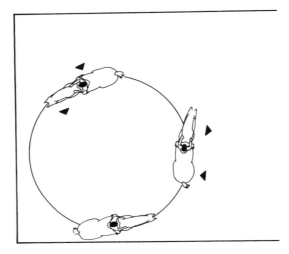

Exercise Five. Use a moment of counter bending to straighten and bring the hindquarters back in line.

Exercise Five: Bending and counter bending.

The short-backed horse will have less ability to bend the spine than the average horse. Consequently, you need to concentrate on loosening the joints of the shoulder and loin.

On circles, take care to keep the hindquarters on the curve behind the forehand. If the horse persists in sliding the hindquarter out, you can correct this by taking the head to the outside for a few steps, which will send the hindquarters in. Ride some steps in this counter-bend, then tactfully bring the head and neck back to the inside, trying to hold the quarters on the correct line. This will take time, and you must change from one position to the other so the horse can develop the ability to step correctly on the curved line.

Exercise Six: The "square serpentine."

To establish control over the placement of the shoulders and to activate the engagement of the hindquarters, you can use a "square serpentine." This is by no means a classical movement, but is a useful one.

Walk the horse down the long side of the arena on the left rein. At some point after the corner, take your outside right leg back behind the girth, turn your own body to the left and bring both hands towards the center of the school. Your right hand will bring the right rein against the neck, while your left hand will lead the horse's head to the left. Your left leg stays closed at the girth. As soon as the horse moves its shoulders two steps off the track, push it forward

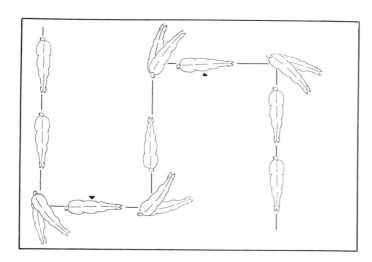

The square serpentine helps free up the shoulders and activates the hindquarters.

with your left leg and ride straight across the school. As you reach the far track repeat the movement, but this time turn the horse to the right.

In effect you are performing two steps of a turn on the haunches and then moving straight. This exercise gives you good control of the shoulders and makes the hindlegs step under the body. It is also an excellent exercise for the rider because it makes you use first one leg, then the other in quick succession and also makes you coordinate your hands with the action of the legs.

You can continue this exercise all round the school. As the horse begins to understand, it will become easier to make the turn and move forward. By the end of a week or so, it will probably be enough merely to move your shoulders and hips in the direction of the turn and the horse will follow your weight. Anything you can do to free up the shoulders will help the horse bend correctly in the direction of the movement. Your aim here is to separate the front end from the back.

The Long Back

The horse with a long back has a different set of difficulties. Often the hindlegs will be far out behind the mass, and the horse must learn to step up under its body. Far from being unable to bend, this type of horse will probably bend too much and in all directions. If the neck is also long, this type can be like a snake to ride; it wiggles along with one end going in one direction and the other in the opposite direction.

Exercise One: The halt.

Your job is to get the hindquarter to come up under the body as much as possible. Ride frequent transitions to the halt, using both your legs slightly behind the girth to drive the hind legs up. When you ask the horse to halt, make sure that it stays straight; there will be a tendency for the hind end to fall to one side

Exercise One, *for long backs. Drive the hindquarter under to halt.*

or the other. If you make your halts alongside the wall or fence, you can easily check which way the horse is crooked. You should be able to counter that tendency by using the leg and rein on that side. For example, if you are going to the right and the horse persistently swings its hindquarters to the left, keep your left leg well back and use your left rein to bring the head and neck slightly left to counter the hindquarters.

All horses are crooked to some degree; your job is to discover where and to ride constructively to correct this. Always ride the horse with the difficulty in mind and you will find the difficulty will eventually disappear. Unfortunately, a brand new one will take its place, but that's the way it goes!

The long-backed horse needs to be carefully balanced and kept straight in all the exercises. I find that teaching the long horse the piaffe early on in its training can help balance it and make it round. I teach it from the ground; see the chapter on piaffe.

Exercise Two: Lateral work.

The lateral work described in chapter 5 helps the long-backed horse to find its center of gravity and should be taught early on in walk and trot. The canter work will present more difficulty and only once the horse has some degree of balance should the canter be worked seriously.

Exercise Three: Hill work.

Changing balance up and down hills helps the long-backed horse develop balance and should be included in the early training program. Riding large serpentine lines on a slope makes the horse shift its weight from front to back and strengthens the muscles. A long back is generally a weak back and needs to be built up.

Exercise Four: "Square serpentine."

The square serpentine exercise mentioned for short-backed horses helps this type also.

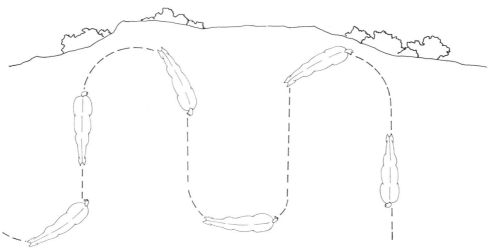

Serpentine hill work, with the changes in balance, improves suppleness.

Exercise Five: Serpentines.

Ordinary curved serpentines with a constant changing of the bend help develop balance and the ability to keep the horse's front and back end aligned. You must be careful to make large loops in the beginning and be strict about the hindquarters staying on the line of the movement without wobbling from side to side. You need to keep your outside leg further back on a long horse than on an average horse, in order to hold all that length in the correct place.

The Loaded Shoulder and/or Short Front Leg

Horses that have straight or heavily muscled shoulders, or horses that have trouble in swinging their shoulders forward tend to be heavy on the forehand. Often a neck that is set on low or a neck that is too short prevents freedom of the shoulders. You need to try and free up the shoulders and shift the load to the hindquarters. These horses tend to "lead" with the shoulder in turns and circles. You must free up the muscles that form the cradle holding the shoulder blades. Extension of the forearm is difficult for these horses, usually making the lengthening of strides quite a problem.

Exercise One: Lateral work in hand.

The work in hand will help loosen and stretch the shoulder muscles. Anytime you ask the horse to cross its front feet, it has to use the shoulder muscles. Slow, careful work in hand loosens the shoulders.

Exercise Two: "Square serpentine."

The value of this universal exercise is the movement of the shoulders during the first two steps. To prevent the horse from falling into the turn with locked shoulders, you can use your whip on the shoulder as you give the aid so that the horse's weight stays central and does not fall on the shoulder.

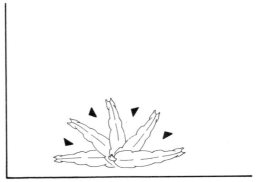

The turn on the haunches.

Exercise Three: The turn on the haunches.

In the turn on the haunches, the aim is to keep the horse stepping behind in the smallest possible circle and having the shoulders move freely. If you have practiced the "square serpentine," you have only to ask the horse to perform four or five steps of the turn instead of two. The rider must bring the outside leg back to anchor the hindquarters, move both hands in the direction of the turn, and keep the inside leg at the girth to keep the bend and impulsion. The horse must move bent in the direction of the turn.

Exercise Four: Cavaletti.

"But cavaletti exercises are for jumpers!" you protest. So they are, but why not use them to solve dressage problems also? If they are good enough for Reiner Klimke to use when he trains, they are good enough for me! You can improve a horse's action by using cavaletti carefully spaced for the purpose.

Trotting through cavaletti makes the horse pick up its feet and improves rhythm and balance.

You place your cavaletti—real cavaletti are better than poles on the ground for this exercise—four feet or so apart, depending upon your horse's length of stride. The cavaletti should be set at about 14 inches so that the horse has to pick its legs up higher than usual. You need six to eight cavaletti to be effective. Let the horse walk through a time or two, then trot over the gymnastic several times each way until the horse develops a round swinging stride. This will help stretch out the locked shoulder muscles because the horse has to lift its feet. You can take this exercise a step further by putting the cavaletti down to the lowest setting but increasing the distance between each so that the horse has to reach farther forward. *Increase the distance very gradually* to prevent strain.

Transitions to and from the halt, using the whip to free up the shoulder.

Exercise Five: Transitions into and out of the halt.

Transitions to and from the halt will help the horse shift its weight and will encourage it to swing forward again. Use your whip on the shoulder to make the horse lift it as it moves forward.

Exercise Six: The piaffe.

Later on the horse will benefit from the roundness developed by the piaffe.

Exercise Seven: Shoulder stretch (for extreme cases).

This exercise is not in the lexicon of classical dressage, but can be used to good effect to open up shoulder muscles. As a gymnastic, it is of great value to both the shoulder and loin muscles. It is taught from the ground.

Stand beside the horse's head facing it and holding the left rein. With your whip tap the horse behind the knee on the left leg, keep this up until the horse stamps its foot. Stop and reward. Repeat.

Once the horse understands that you want it to pick up its foot, the next stage is to persuade it to extend the leg forward and to step onto that leg. This

Teaching the shoulder stretch exercise.

can take time. You may have to keep up a relentless tapping behind the knee or on the tendon so the horse will try to avoid the whip by throwing its leg up and out in front. Once you get this reaction, praise it and quit for the day.

The next day, begin all over. But this time, stand by the horse's head, facing backwards. Once the horse gestures forward with the leg, step backwards yourself and tug the rein to bring the horse a step forward. The horse must throw the leg up and out, then step onto it at full extension. Some horses have difficulty in extending the leg forward and will persist in bending the knee. Keep tapping behind the fetlock with the whip until the horse reaches out. Work on one leg at a time and keep at it until you can walk down the side of the school with the horse lifting the leg nearest to you at each step. This can take several days.

Now turn the horse around and begin all over. Just because the horse has cottoned on to the idea of lifting its left leg, it will not necessarily relate that to lifting the right leg so you must go back to step one. When it has learned to lift and step forward with the second leg, you then must coordinate both legs.

Stand beside the horse facing it and tap the leg nearest to you. As the horse brings that leg up, tap the leg furthest away from you. After some practice the horse will lift one leg then the other and will "goose step" two to three consecutive steps. Praise it effusively.

I have used this exercise on perhaps five horses for one reason or another and, frankly, have always been terrified that it would come back to haunt me in the show ring. However, it has served its purpose for all of these animals with problems in their shoulders and loins. Extreme problems sometimes require extreme solutions!

Neck Problems

The horse with a thick short neck will have trouble in bending and using the neck without taking the shoulder in the same direction. The exercises for unmounted and mounted flexions to the sides can help free up and stretch the

SHORT   **LONG**   **EWE**

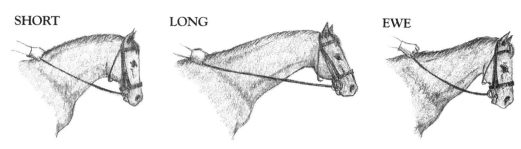

Necks; short, long, ewe

neck muscles. Counter-bending on large circles, followed by correct bending, can be helpful. You have to keep as much neck out in front of you as possible and must not, under any circumstance, shorten the neck by using too much rein contact. You may have to sacrifice a little of the head position so that the horse can use its neck to balance itself. A short thick neck usually means a thick throatlatch as well and if you ask for too vertical a position of the head, you can actually cut off the horse's air supply and it will cough or choke.

The long neck has to be carefully stabilized; otherwise, it wiggles around and upsets the balance of the whole horse. You need to keep a steady contact but, again, do not try and shorten the neck to do this. If you do, you will only cause resistance elsewhere. Encourage the horse to move forward towards its head and be sure to keep a steady hand on each rein. As the neck muscles develop, the head will stabilize gradually. Try to avoid overbending the neck.

The ewe neck can be improved by careful muscle-building exercises such as lungeing, stretching exercises, and by careful "strapping." Strapping is part of the grooming routine. You take a cloth or stable mitt and slap smartly on the muscles on top of the neck. This causes the horse to contract and relax the muscles, just like an isometric exercise, and you can radically develop muscle over a period of six months or so. If you religiously bang at least twenty times on each upper muscle once or twice a day, you will soon be able to see the results. Dressage, after all, is gymnastics and gymnastics build muscles, as do massage and isometrics.

A word here about "frame." To me "frame" denotes something rigid and fixed. There is no such thing as a "First Level Frame" or a "Second Level Frame," but only the carriage of each horse at each level of training. The word has come into use because it is used on the F.E.I. tests as a poor translation of the original French word *"l'encloure."* *L'encloure* includes the head and neck from the withers up — the entire superstructure in front. A better translation would be "posture," "carriage" or "bearing." As each horse's conformation differs, so will each horse's self carriage differ from the next. Don't fall into the trap of trying to place the head and neck in a preconceived position; let the horse's head *take a natural position in relation to the engagement of the hindquarters.* Many of the problems in dressage training seen nowadays stem from riders who try to fix the front end instead of the back end. If you take care to get the back end in gear, the front end will fall into place naturally and easily.

Don't force the neck into a set position, just let the horse stretch forward to the bit. As the hindquarters become more active and bend, the neck will assume the best position to balance them. The horse is like a spring; press the back end under and support the front, so that you obtain an arching of the spine.

Stiffness and Crookedness

Some horses are born stiff, some achieve stiffness and some have stiffness thrust upon them. The same applies to crookedness. Whatever the reason, your job is to work through the problem and teach the horse to use all its joints and muscles. Age makes a difference: the stiff, crooked five year old can be redeemed, the stiff fifteen year old can be improved but only to a certain extent. Its muscles have been set in youth and will only give so much.

There are two schools of thought when it comes to correcting the crooked horse: the "Flexionist school" and the "Impulsionist school." Both have the same goal—to straighten the horse and to create equal thrust from each hind leg by working the muscles on both sides. In other words, you can "bend 'em" or "send 'em."

The bending school works on the theory that if you bend a horse to the left, you are stretching the muscles on the right side of the horse, and vice versa. The exercises used by this school are suited to horses that have good natural impulsion such as thoroughbreds, arabs, anglo-arabs—the lighter, more nervous animals.

The impulsion school believes that the horse must be chased strongly forward onto the bit before you can begin to straighten it. This works best for the more phlegmatic, heavier type of horses such as most warmbloods, half-breds, and horses with a dose of cold blood.

In reality, I find myself using some of the exercises from one school and some from the other; it just depends on the horse.

You must decide first what type of horse you are dealing with and, next, where it is crooked or stiff. The exercises that are designed to work on a horse that is crooked to the left will not help the horse that is crooked to the right; in fact, they will make it worse. In the early days of training, it is sometimes difficult to decide where the crookedness lies. The young horse will not have good balance and may well seem crooked when it is only weak. Often when you work hard on straightening one side of the horse, lo and behold—a couple of weeks later you will find it has developed crookedness on the other side!

The "bend 'em" exercises: (at walk and trot)

a. Use an inverse rotation with the right leg behind the girth to move the quarters around the shoulders to the left, with the left leg at the girth to push the horse to the bit. The horse's head should be placed slightly left to stretch the right side.

b. Use a direct rotation with the shoulders moving outside the hindquarters, with the right leg at the girth, left leg back, and the horse flexed to the left.

c. Make a volte (small 6-meter circle) to the left with the horse bent to the left (stretched on the right).

d. Make a volte to the right with the horse bent to the left.

e. Use a left shoulder-in.

f. Ride a quarters-in to the left on a volte.

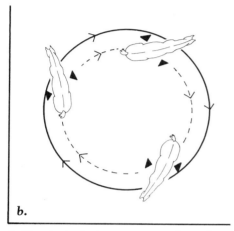

b.

In Exercise b, the horse moves on the circle with the hindquarters to the inside, and the shoulders moving on a larger circle, bent away from the direction of the movement.

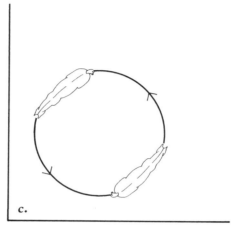

c.

Volte to the left, with horse bent to the left.

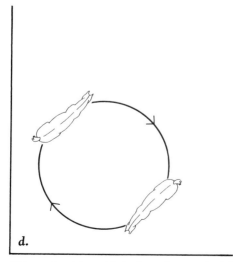

d.

Volte to the right, with the horse bent to the left.

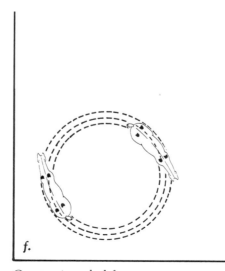

f.

Quarters-in to the left.

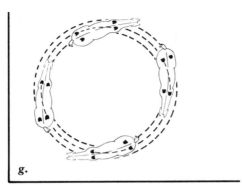

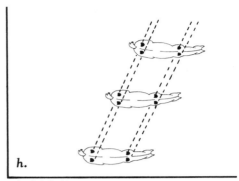

Quarters-in to the left, with left shoulder-in.   *The left half pass.*

    g. Ride a quarters-in to the left alternating with left shoulder-in.

    h. Practice a left half pass.

    If the horse does not engage one hind leg as much as the other, use shoulder-in and half pass on that side.

    The "bend 'em" exercises at the canter can be done after the horse can easily perform the walk and trot work.

    a. Canter left on the circle with the horse bent to the circle.

    b. Canter right on a circle while bent to the left.

    c. Canter on a serpentine without changing lead or bend.

    d. Counter-canter on a circle to the left with right leg leading, but bent left.

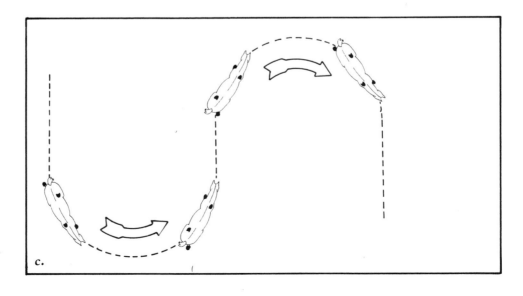

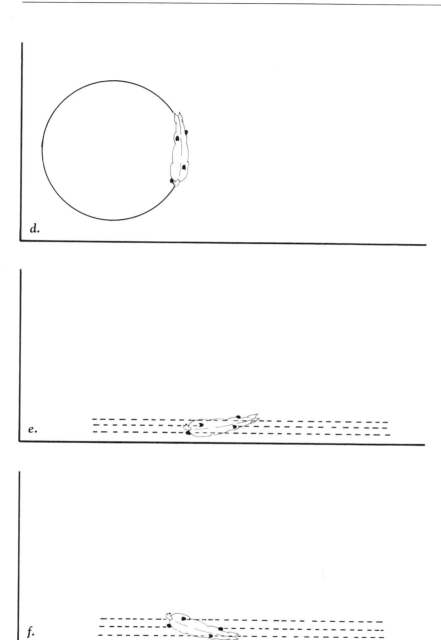

e. Left shoulder-in at canter.

f. Canter with the horse's head to the wall and the quarters inside the track in left lead.

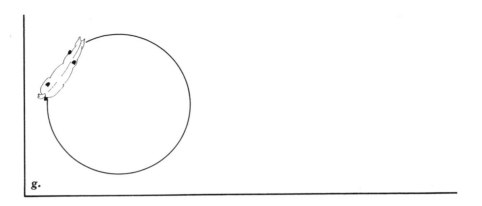

g.

g. Counter-canter to the right with the left leg leading and bent left.

The canter is useful in correcting the crooked horse as the horse has a natural tendency to be slightly crooked in this gait.

The "send 'em" school first gets the horse moving forward with strong impulsion, with a strong contact on the bit and driving the horse up towards the bit. Then they use the following exercises:

At the walk:

  a. Circle to the right on a small circle, using the right rein towards the shoulder to oppose the quarters and send them to the left outside the circle. This also helps to make the horse learn to take the right rein.

  b. Ride a left shoulder-in on a large circle to the left, sending the horse towards the right rein. This is similar to the "bend 'em" theories.

  c. Once the horse has taken the contact with the right rein in exercise a, use a direct right rein and an indirect left rein to bend him to the left while still on the small circle to the right.

At the trot:

  a. All three of these exercises that you used at the walk can be done in a short energetic trot with as much energy as you can get.

  b. Ride a lengthening of the trot in between turns to the right. For example, turn to the right across the school, ask the horse to lengthen. On reaching the far side, turn the horse to the right, using the right rein strongly to send the hindquarters left. At the same time use the left rein towards the shoulder to straighten the horse.

  c. Use leg-yielding, the turns on the forehand and hindquarters, and rotations on the circle to control and engage the weak hindleg.

As soon as the horse gets lighter on the left rein, it must be sent firmly forward so that it keeps the contact and accepts an even feel on both reins.

At the canter:

    a. In right canter (crooked side)
        i. Without losing contact with the right rein, use the outside rein to bring the shoulders into the circle and spiral in.
        ii. Ask for a slightly longer stride and spiral out again using the right leg and keeping an open right rein.

    b. In left canter (the opposite side to the crookedness)
        i. Use shoulder-in on a large circle.
        ii. Use shoulder-in on a large circle, make the circle larger and reduce it again.
        iii. Using the right rein towards the rear, in opposition to the quarters, ride a circle to the left with the quarters inside the circle.

If the horse does not accept a contact on the bit, the legs must drive him firmly forward. Sometimes as the horse begins to become straight it will avoid contact with one rein. If so, ride small circles using a strong inside rein and throw the quarters outside the circle. When the horse accepts the rein on this side, reverse the direction and put the quarters inside the circle again.

These exercises sound a little confusing, but as you practice you will find that they are effective for some horses. It is up to you to decide which system or which exercises will be most effective. To ride a horse straight is perhaps the most difficult task in dressage—it is the real challenge.

With the older horse that is really stiff you need to take the time on the lunge line and with the work in hand before trying these exercises. The loosening exercises and the lateral work will help the stiff horse. The "bend 'em" exercises are more suited but keep the rhythm painfully slow until the horse is able to move more freely; then worry about impulsion. If you force a stiff horse into moving forward before its muscles are relaxed, you run the risk of damage—a tight muscle will tear or pull. Your job is to stretch muscles and make them elastic, then go vigorously forward.

Temperament

No matter what conformation the horse possesses, none of its physical ability can be effectively used if the temperament is unsuitable. Horses fall into two general groups: those who are nervous and quick, and those who are sluggish and stubborn. There are, of course, thousands of graduations of each type.

The extremely nervous horse that flies off at the slightest pretext may be a horse that has been badly started and frightened in the early stages of training. If you can gain its confidence, it becomes trainable. On the other hand, the slow-to-react horse needs to be motivated. Once in a while you will encounter a third type: the horse that really dislikes people and fights back. Fortunately, these are rare; they are dangerous and best left to really experienced trainers. Generally speaking, bad horses are few and far between.

With the nervous horse, you need time and the utmost patience. Retraining begins in the stable with the everyday care of the animal. Take the time to reassure the horse each time you approach it; have a ready supply of goodies to win its trust.

Exercise One: The lesson of the whip.

Before you even begin to lunge the horse it must accept the whip. It may have been frightened by a whip early on; if so, you must reeducate its mind so it can accept the whip as an aid and not a punishment. I often have students say "My horse won't let me carry a whip." Who then is training who?

Stand by the horse after tacking up and show it the lunge whip. Let the horse sniff the whip and feed a tidbit. Gently rub the horse's nose with the butt end of the whip while keeping up a soothing chatter. Progress to the side of the neck. If the horse flinches or runs back snorting violently, hold the rein firmly and bring it to a halt, and start over. *Take your time.* It pays to be thorough at this point; what is one or two days' patience compared to the rest of the training schedule of three or four years? Everyone is in too much of a hurry; there is no instant dressage. Time spent at the beginning makes the later work go quickly.

If the horse persists in running from the whip, stand it against the wall in the corner to prevent this. For the first day it would be sufficient if you could rub the neck, shoulders and front legs on each side before going about the lungeing routine. When you do lunge this type of horse, use the whip sparingly and keep your movements slow and methodical. No cracking the whip for the first sessions.

If you have success in this first session, repeat all the moves the next day, and try to rub the flanks and belly. Keep reinforcing with "goodies" and keep talking. If the horse accepts being groomed, it can learn to accept the touch of the whip. Horses in nature groom each other; touching is natural to them.

Once the horse accepts the touch of the lunge whip all over the body, you can then do the same with a dressage whip to prepare the horse for the work in hand. If your work in hand is correct, the horse should lose its fear and you will be able to carry your whip when mounted.

When you mount, repeat the exercise of rubbing the horse all over its body with the whip before you let it walk forward. If you persist in this way most horses will come to realize that the whip is just part of the routine. I can give no exact timetable for this work but it is worth the time spent because you are establishing your authority over the horse—a vital element in its training, no matter how nervous.

Exercise Two: The lesson of the leg.

Hand in glove, or rather, foot in stirrup, with the first exercise is the problem of getting the nervous horse to accept your leg without shooting off. If you cannot use your leg, you have no chance of training the horse to do anything. It is a grave error to take your leg off a horse that runs from the leg. You must keep the leg close; otherwise, what happens when you put it on? The horse runs away again.

When you first mount, wrap your leg around the horse and keep it there. To move forward into walk, tighten the muscle of your calves and use the same voice command you use while lungeing. Relax the leg *as soon as* the horse moves but *keep the leg close.* To move up to trot, use the same pressure with both legs.

The horse must accept the touch of the whip all over.

If the horse ignores you, tap it, every so gently, with the dreaded whip. If the horse leaps forward, allow it to run for several steps before bringing it back and starting over. Be patient; let the horse go and bring it back again and again — don't give up. Keep at it until the horse gives in and accepts a light pressure to move forward.

Use the same routine for the canter depart after you have the walk and trot transitions down pat. It takes extreme tact to ride a sensitive horse, but it can be the most rewarding since, when controlled, you have only to think about things for them to happen. The skill lies in being able to use the lightest of aids without upsetting the horse.

I also use my voice a great deal with nervous horses. Sometimes, I'll set up "frightening" situations in the home arena and make sure that the horse is exposed to all manner of confusion and noise. With one young nervous horse, before we went off to the first schooling show, I took him to a friend's for a lesson. I brought along his owners, my stable crew and assorted pupils who sat on the edge of the arena and whopped, banged chairs, and jumped up and down. My instructor said "My God! If my horses tolerated that commotion, I would be more than happy." When we did get to the show he won his first dressage class (even though he almost held his breath throughout because of the strangeness of the ring). Doing your homework with the nervous horse pays off.

After you have established a good rapport with the horse, you must get to the stage where you can dominate so that it pays more attention to you than to whatever outside demons may exist. The more control you establish at home, the more control you will have away. Make the horse respect the whip and your leg, and you are on the road to obedience.

To me the ultimate in dressage training is represented by a film taken during the warm up for one of the Olympic tests. A horse is being schooled in piaffe in the warm-up ring when a sheet of newspaper, a double sheet, blows across the ring and wraps around one foreleg. The newspaper unwraps and blows away but the horse never misses a beat—what attention and confidence!

The super nervous horse is certainly not for everyone but if you have time and patience, it can become an honest, hardworking partner. Remember that nervousness is often the direct result of uneducated handling early on.

The dull or "thick" horse needs to be strongly motivated in order to train it. Here again it needs to learn the lesson of the whip, but it must learn that it must jump when you use it. Don't hesitate to get after this type from the beginning; far from frightening it, you may have to galvanize it into action. Some horses do not realize that they have to work for their feed.

Again, you want the horse to move from a light aid. You must reinforce your aids with sharp taps of the whip until the horse gives in and moves promptly from your leg. To me this type of horse is not as interesting as the other, but both can benefit from the time spent getting them to concentrate and respond.

Mouth Problems

Perhaps the most difficult of all problems to resolve are those horses that have difficulties in their mouths. These difficulties are usually from poor management in breaking, but some horses do have problem mouths because of the actual structure.

The horse that opens its mouth and drops the contact, avoiding the bit, can be helped with the use of a dropped or flash noseband, although you do not want to be too quick in resorting to one. Often the young horse will learn to accept the bit as training progresses and it seems a shame to use restraint when time will solve the problem. Both types of noseband, if fitted too tightly, can cause the horse to clench its jaw and lean and contract its muscles.

Some horses will go better in a straight bit than in a jointed one if their mouths are difficult. A general rule of thumb is to use a milder bit when you find resistance, not a harsher one.

For the horse that puts its tongue over the bit, you will have to find a solution that does not aggravate the resistance. Some horses with small mouths just don't have room for a thick bit. In this case, a thinner (more severe) bit may fit. You can use a tongue port, a rubber gadget that fits over the joint of the snaffle and depresses the tongue, but remember this is only a temporary solution and forbidden in competition.

Have the horse's teeth checked at least twice a year. Frequently, mouth problems arise from sharp teeth and a dentist can work wonders. If there is no visible physical reason for mouth resistance, turn your attention to the back and hindquarters. With the horse moving in balance and engaged, mouth problems will probably disappear.

For horses that have chronic mouth problems, you are better off seeking the help of a professional. Frankly, the best advice I can give is to get another horse. A horse with a problem mouth will never bring happiness, no matter how talented. It will always be worrying about its mouth and not about what you want it to do. I know—I had one and he broke my heart.

◇8◇
CANTER WORK

Canter is the odd man out of the three gaits since it has an uneven beat and the legs do not move symetrically. In the wild, horses rarely trot; they spend much of their time walking and grazing and use the canter or gallop when threatened. It is important to understand the mechanics of the canter before you start to work on developing a good balance.

In the early stage be content to let the horse canter on the lunge and find its balance on the circle. Circles will do more to balance the canter in the beginning than any mounted work. Under the rider, the horse should learn to strike off on a given lead from the trot, and be allowed to make a downward transition with minimum use of the rein. If you try to bring the horse down from the canter with too strong a rein contact, you teach the horse to drop onto its forehand and to rely on the rein during the transition. Thoroughbreds off the track have been taught to rely on a strong support from the reins; you have to wean them from that idea and teach them to make a downward transition from the hindquarters to balance themselves.

The horse has to be taught to carry the weight from behind. The greater speed of the canter causes a natural tendency to drop the weight forward.

The mechanics of the canter are briefly discussed in the lungeing section of chapter 2 but are worth looking at briefly again. The canter is a three-beat gait with a moment of suspension, making four stages in all. The horse's spine has a natural bend towards the outside hind leg, the leg that is providing impulsion, while the head and neck counterbalance this by drifting to the outside. Watching horses galloping loose in the field, you'll notice they lead with the shoulders in turns.

If the horse has a very unbalanced canter, it will need lots of lunge work using transitions until it learns to shift its weight to the rear. Cantering up and down slopes also helps to balance the horse, as long as you don't let it barrel downhill or charge uphill as if it were with Teddy Roosevelt at San Juan. Keep a steady rhythm.

The first beat in the left lead canter, as the right hind comes through and pushes the mass forward.

The second beat of the canter. The right hind is still on the ground, with the left hind and right fore also on the ground. The left fore is about to touch the ground.

The leading leg is about to hit the ground. The inside hind is really engaged so the horse is able to remain light in front.

The moment of suspension, before the right hind hits the ground and begins the next canter stride.

Some horses have great difficulty at the canter in the beginning. Since this problem usually stems from a physical weakness, you must study the horse and analyze the difficulty. Some horses persist in cross-cantering, usually more on one lead than the other; this is due to uneven muscle development. Some horses get very excited by the canter. All of these problems must be dealt with in the beginning because later, when you want to teach different exercises in canter, the horse may well revert to the early behavior.

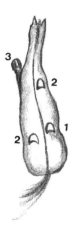

When cantering free, the horse has a tendency to balance by leaning away from the leading leg.

The horse that has trouble with one lead needs to be worked on the lunge as described in the lungeing chapter. If the horse can learn to take both leads on the lunge, it can learn to take them when mounted.

If the horse has trouble taking the right lead when asked, you have several options. You can ride the horse deep into the corner and ask for the depart, leading the horse with the inside rein held out and the outside rein held upwards to send the shoulders over. With your left leg well back, ask for canter as the left diagonal is in support. The left hind must provide the thrust into canter.

You can also try riding the horse straight across the school perpendicular to the wall and, in the last yard before reaching the wall, turn the head to the right and ask for the depart.

If these methods fail, you can attempt bending the head and neck to the outside and letting the horse fall onto the inside shoulder. This is only a last resort, however, and should only be used until the lead has been established.

As another option, you can reduce the size of the circle and ride a tiny circle in the corner and ask for the depart as you get back to the wall. Sometimes, placing a pole on the ground in the corner and asking for the depart as you reach the pole works wonders.

Whatever method you use, once you get the lead send the horse forward and praise it and pat it effusively. It should not take longer than a week to confirm the leads.

The horse that is gifted with a balanced canter can progress much more rapidly to the more complicated exercises. The horse with a poor canter needs lots of time to develop its balance.

The downward transitions should be into a forward trot at this point. If you ride the transition by shifting your weight onto the outside seatbone and blocking the outside hindleg, the horse should be able to change from canter to trot without hurrying and without falling on the forehand. At first, ride these transitions after a circle going down the long side. Then you can begin to ride the horse across the diagonal of the school, ride the transition to trot, and pick up the new canter lead at the end of the diagonal. Make sure the horse remains perfectly straight both in the downward transition and particularly in the upward one to the new lead. Don't let the horse fall around the corner into canter. From the very beginning, the horse must learn to do a straight canter depart.

Try also to ride the canter depart in the middle or at the beginning of the long side instead of in the corner. Hone your skills and practice so the horse can depart to canter anywhere at the slightest touch.

Once the horse can canter along the wall and around a large circle at the ends and the middle of the school, you are ready to think about counter-canter. I believe that the earlier you teach the counter-canter the better. If you wait too long, the horse will be reluctant to take the "wrong" lead, and you may have brought trouble upon yourself. If the horse can maintain a rhythm down both sides and on the circle, it is ready.

As a introduction to the counter canter, ride a loop towards **X** *and back to the track again.*

Counter-canter can be taught by using several techniques. Perhaps the best introduction is to canter a shallow loop down the long side. Put the horse in left lead canter, ride through the short end, and start towards X. Before reaching the center line, gradually push the horse back towards the track again and continue to the left. Pat the horse! If the horse breaks gait on the first attempt, try again and be sure you are not shifting your own weight. The horse remains *bent to the leading leg;* do not change the position of the head and neck as you make the loop back to the wall and don't shift your weight to the right. If you stay centered, the horse has a much easier job.

For the horse that is obedient in the canter depart, you can turn down the quarter line of the school, push the horse towards the wall, and ask for the outside lead. Continue down the wall, making a transition to trot before the corner to prevent an attempt to change. Try both these methods on both leads. If you get a good response the first time, leave it at that for the first day. Go back and repeat the next day. Let the horse accept the idea of the "wrong" lead but don't make a big deal of it. A little success now leads to greater success later on.

Gradually increase the length of the counter-canter phase until you feel the horse is in good balance. Then, sitting very lightly, almost pushing your seat up off the saddle, let the horse continue on through the short end. Many riders think that the counter-canter is difficult and make it so by tightening up and anticipating trouble. If you make a big change in your aids, the horse will instinctively think something is up. *Counter-canter ridden in balance is not difficult, don't make it so!* Once through the short end, ride a transition to trot and make a big fuss of the horse.

Later, when you can successfully ride through the short end, ride back across the diagonal and continue in true canter. But don't try for this the first few times;

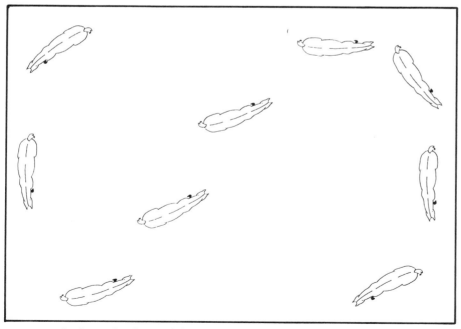

Canter across the diagonal and around the short end in counter canter. Later on, turn back to cross the diagonal again to the true lead.

the turn from the corner to the diagonal in counter-canter is too demanding for the beginning lessons.

Counter-canter will improve the true canter 100 percent as the horse develops balance and suppleness. Counter-canter works directly on the loins and brings many benefits in its wake, including increased obedience.

Continue perfecting the counter-canter as you go about your daily routine. Your aim is to be able to put the horse on either lead in either direction at any time you so desire. Progress until you can ride large circles in both true canter and counter-canter, and ride large serpentines on both leads without changing the rhythm or laboring.

The horse that has a balanced canter can begin to do the exercise of decreasing and increasing the circle in canter early on. For the unbalanced horse, it is best to wait until the balance improves with the counter-canter. If you try a smaller circle and the horse loses balance or begins to labor up and down, it is not ready and needs more suppleness. Anytime the horse stops its forward momentum, it must be sent forward again until it can keep its balance in the more demanding exercises.

Frequent transitions between a lengthened canter and a slightly shorter canter help drive the hind end up under the body. For the horse that has a really horrible canter you do not want to stay in canter for a long time. Instead, you should ride literally thousands of transitions from trot to canter and back into trot. If the horse has trouble with its balance or is excessively on the forehand, don't just run on and let things deteriorate. Come back to trot and restart until the hind end develops the ability to come under the mass.

For the excitable horse, cantering ad infinitum on the circle will eventually calm it down. Let it canter around and around with little or no rein contact so that it has to find its own balance; don't haul on the reins to support it. As a desperate measure, you can take both reins upwards near your nose and hold them there as the horse rushes on. A horse can only pull forward; it cannot pull downward. By taking the reins upwards, you remove the temptation to pull and run.

When the canter is balanced and regular, and the transitions to and from the trot are prompt and reliable, you can advance to making transitions to canter from the walk and from canter back to the walk. The timing of the aids becomes twice as important in this work. For the horse to make clear-cut, clean transitions, you must be crystal clear with your aids. The work you are doing now prepares the horse for correct flying changes without difficulty later on, so the time you spend on this will be well spent.

I don't understand why the timing of the aids is not taught in riding schools. I spent years learning to ride but no one ever really discussed the timing of the aids; they just said "do this and this," but never explained why. It is much easier to understand and to give aids correctly if you understand the mechanics of why they work.

To make a canter depart from the walk, the horse has to engage its outside hindleg, which then lifts the entire body up into canter. Canter is *not* a matter of just going faster. A horse can canter from the walk, from a reinback and from

To depart from the walk, the horse must be able to engage the outside hind and elevate the forehand.

the halt, so it stands to reason it does not have to trot fast and fall into canter.

Given the footfalls in walk—right front, left hind, left front, right hind—you must consider the footfalls in the canter so you can ask for the depart at the moment when the horse's legs are in position to strike off promptly. In left canter, the right hind leg provides the thrust, followed by the right fore and left hind diagonal together, then the "leading" leg, the left fore. In the walk, as the left fore swings forward, apply your right leg behind the girth and your left leg at the girth. Take a deep breath, lift your ribcage (don't lean forward), and the horse will canter. Even better, the horse will go cleanly into canter without shuffling its feet. If your timing is off, the horse has to rearrange its feet until it is in a position to depart, and this makes for a "blurred" strike off. You want the horse to move directly from the walk to canter with no interim steps.

Exercises for the canter depart are:

Canter from trot.

Canter from walk.

Canter from rein back.

Canter from halt.

Canter from half-pirouette.

Canter a circle from a shoulder-in at walk down the wall.

Canter depart from half pass in walk to the center line.

Canter depart to a counter canter, from the half pass begun on the center line.

Change of lead through the trot, across the school.

Simple change of lead, canter-walk-canter.

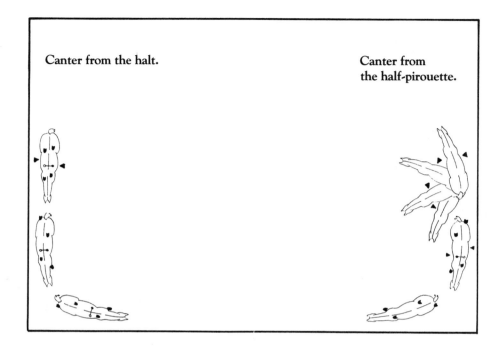

Canter from the halt.

Canter from
the half-pirouette.

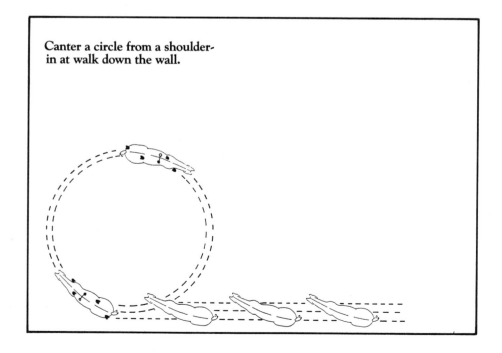

Canter a circle from a shoulder-
in at walk down the wall.

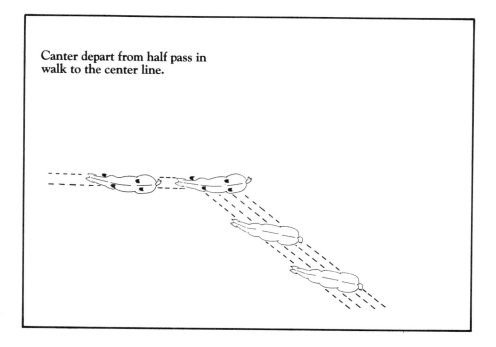

Canter depart from half pass in
walk to the center line.

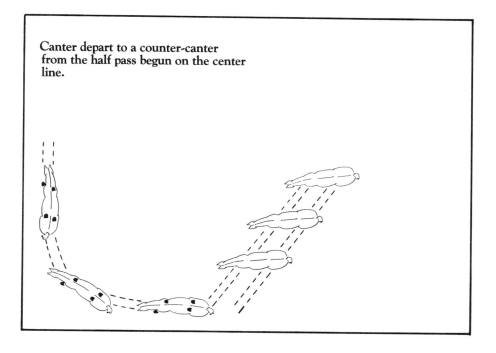

Canter depart to a counter-canter
from the half pass begun on the center
line.

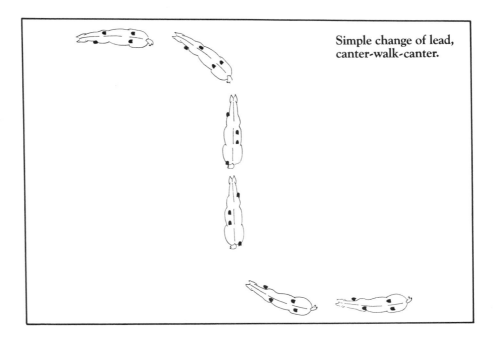

Simple change of lead, canter-walk-canter.

Refine your canter departs until they are automatic.

During this same period of training, work on getting a clean canter to walk transition. If you have been careful with your canter to trot transitions and have not let the horse develop the habit of falling onto the forehand in the downward transition, the next step should be relatively easy.

As you ride the canter, you follow the swing of the horse's back with your own back. In the left canter, you swing your left hip towards the pommel with each stride with your right leg remaining closed behind the girth and your left leg at the girth, with both legs relaxed. In the transition from canter to walk, as the horse places its leading leg on the ground, you should shift your weight from the left seatbone to the right seatbone, sharply and very definitely; think of blocking the right hind leg. At the same time, close your right hand on the outside rein, and sink down into the saddle with your back held stiff for a split second. This is the same aid you have been using in the canter to trot transition but intensified and stronger. The horse should walk. At first you may get one or two steps of trot, but keep at it until the horse comes down flatfooted, or directly into the walk with no bouncing steps or half trot steps. The horse should move cleanly into a walk stride from the hindquarter and walk steadily forward with no loss of balance. You don't want canter—stop—walk, you want canter—walk, so as soon as you have given the aid, you must relax and allow the horse to move forward instantly.

Practice these transitions all around the school. Your aim is to be able to strike off on either leg at any time in any place and to be able to return to the walk on demand. Once you can do this confidently, the horse is beginning to be finely tuned, like a sports car.

Along with this work on transitions, you should be benefitting from the work in counter-canter and the horse should be better and better balanced.

You should also be working on getting the medium and extended canter and transitions back and forth in the canter itself, not just working from gait to gait.

A ground-covering medium canter, stretched and relaxed.

Using the horse's natural tendency to bend to the outside in canter, you can allow just a little outwards flexion of the neck in lengthening the canter. Let the horse stretch out with a slight bend to the outside to increase the length of the stride, and compress and straighten it to collect the stride. It works wonders!

As the canter improves, you can begin to ride smaller circles either inside the large circle or at some point on the long side. When the canter is balanced and regular, you can start the lateral work in the canter.

Shoulder-in at the canter makes the horse straight and puts the hindquarters well under the mass. You need ask for only a slight angle in the beginning as most horses have trouble in bringing the shoulders in. The half pass in canter is easier to teach than in the trot, but you must be careful not to let the quarters fall to the inside. Haunches-in and haunches-out in counter-canter will increase engagement as does work in the half pass position on the circles.

Half pass in canter improves balance and collection.

The rider keeps the weight in the direction of the movement. The horse opens the shoulder and covers ground sideways and forward.

From collected canter, bend the horse slightly to the outside for medium or extended canter, and then back to the inside bend to collect again.

The half-pirouette in walk is closely allied to the half-pirouette in canter, so let's look first at the walk. The first lesson in walk is the square serpentine using a quarter turn on the inside and straight on. The horse should now be ready

to perform a half-pirouette, or half-turn on the haunches. The difference between the two forms is that the half-turn on the haunches is ridden in working
walk and the half-pirouette in collected walk. If your horse has a walk that tends
to get "pacey," forget about collected walk until the horse is really advanced in
training. Many walks have been ruined because they have been overshortened
too soon and the horse locks up its back and swings the legs in lateral pairs.

The first half-turns on the haunches can be ridden with the hindquarters
making a small half-circle. The important point is to keep the rhythm of the walk;
the inside hind leg must keep stepping in time. The horse must not plant the
hind feet and swing the forehand around, twisting behind.

Sit straight on the horse with your left leg (for the left turn) on the girth
urging the inside hind to step. Your right leg goes behind the girth to anchor
the right hind and to prevent it from stepping out sideways in the turn. Your

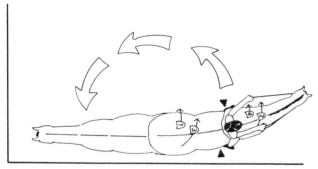

The aids for the half-pirouette.

left hand leads the forehand to the left, and the right hand stays by the shoulders
to bring them around. The horse remains bent to the left.

The most common fault is losing control of the hindquarters so that when
the turn is finished, the horse has moved several feet off the track. The turn must
begin and finish on the track. The horse and rider should look in the direction
of the movement. The rider must take care not to leave the weight over the right
leg as it is taken back because that would be in effect telling the horse to move
to the left but to stay to the right at the same time.

The aids and the balance for this turn are exactly the same as the aids and
the balance for the half- and full pirouette in canter. Once the horse knows the
half-pirouette in walk, you can ask for a complete 360 degree pirouette in walk
on a large circle.

Pirouettes in canter are not often performed well in dressage tests. The troubles
most often seen are loss of rhythm and balance, and an excessive bobbing up
and down of the entire horse. A good pirouette must appear effortless and cadenced
with the horse well seated on the hindquarter, keeping the canter strides as it
turns. Very careful preparation and the time spent in the early stages make for
successful pirouettes. Again, this is a difficult exercise and the rider tends to "clutch,"

thinking "this is difficult." But as soon as the rider transmits that message to the horse, the pirouette is doomed.

Before attempting a pirouette, the canter must be collected and balanced with well defined steps, and the hindlegs jumping through and coming up under the center of the mass. Unless the horse is well seated on the hindquarters, it cannot perform a good pirouette.

Several preparatory exercises help develop a rhythmic pirouette. You can begin by reducing the size of the circles in canter until you can bring the horse onto a small volte without a loss of impulsion or cadence. Circles ridden in haunches-

The horse needs to be a little more engaged or "seated" for the beginning of the pirouette.

Better balance. The horse is supporting the weight behind, not being pulled around by the rein.

in also help seat the horse. You can ride a square in canter: ride to the end of the school, bring the forehand to the inside for two steps and ride straight forward to the other side of the school. Repeat the two steps. Be sure to keep your shoulders back and your upper body stretched up. Your head turns in the direction of the movement, but you must not tip your weight to the inside. The horse's outside leg has to bear the weight and if you load its inside shoulder, the horse will fall in and be unable to keep its balance. Too many riders get anxious about turning to the inside and unbalance their horses so the pirouette becomes impossible. Your outside leg anchors the outside hind and the forehand must come up in front of you and move to the inside. By taking just two steps in the early stages, you learn to keep the impulsion and forward feeling that is vital for the execution of a good pirouette, and you learn the use of the inside leg which is also vital for success.

Another way is to ask for the pirouette well away from the confines of the walls, pick up the canter immediately, and ask for a quarter or half-pirouette in canter. Canter forward on a circle. Return to walk and praise the horse.

To prepare for the pirouette, ride a square in canter. Canter straight, ride two steps of pirouette, and then straight forward again.

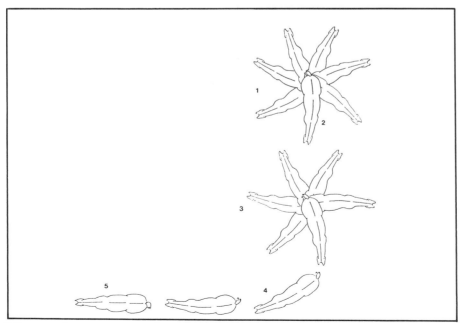

1, Ride a complete pirouette in walk; 2, canter; 3, ride a canter pirouette; 4, ride forward; and 5, down the track.

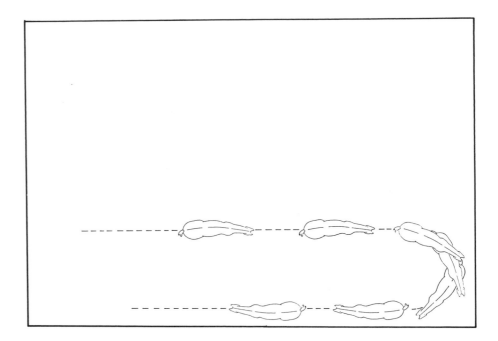

Another good preparation, as shown above, is to ride in counter-canter down the quarter line, turn the horse in a small half-circle towards the corner at the end and continue back the way you came. The wall helps the horse to remain seated on the hindquarters.

A pirouette is a real test of the rider's tact since the horse must remain calm and light throughout. The rider must look to the inside without overloading the inside shoulder, and must not be anxious and try to use the inside rein forcefully. The inside rein acts at the beginning of the pirouette to give the indication of the direction and then should be relaxed to allow the horse to carry itself through the turn. The outside rein brings the forehand around.

The inside leg plays an important part in keeping the bend and the rhythm of the canter in the pirouette, and serves to send the horse forward again upon completion.

Ideally, the pirouette should be composed of six to eight canter strides. During the pirouette, the canter needs the highest degree of collection.

The key to a good pirouette is the perfection of the collected canter. Be sure your horse can carry itself lightly and in excellent balance before you consider teaching even the half-pirouette. This is an exercise that will be developed in the second or third year of training and does not belong in the early exercises. A pirouette demands great strength and agility. If you ask before the horse has sufficient muscle development, you will create too much stress.

The horse in self carriage and perfect balance in the pirouette. The rider carries the whip, with reins light, in the fashion of de la Gueriniere.

Flying changes

Some horses are born to do flying changes, but those with poorly defined canters will need all the help you can give them.

From the beginning of your work on the lunge, watch the canter work. The horse with an exceptional canter will probably offer a flying change if it happens to strike off on the outside lead and switches to keep its balance. The horse that persists in cross-cantering will be a difficult pupil when you get to the changes. Be forewarned by your observations.

When the horse can make nice clear cut transitions from canter to walk and can depart perfectly straight into the canter from the walk anywhere in the school anytime you ask, either to true canter or counter-canter, even on a large circle, you can begin to teach the flying changes.

By this time you will have discovered the horse's "best" lead, so it stands to reason that you want to ask for the change to that lead first. If the right canter is more balanced than the left, you want to ask for a change from left to right, and vice versa.

If the horse is well prepared it can perform a flying change easily from a light aid. Often horses become excited in the flying changes because the riders, thinking "this is more difficult," use strong emphatic aids and upset the horse. If the

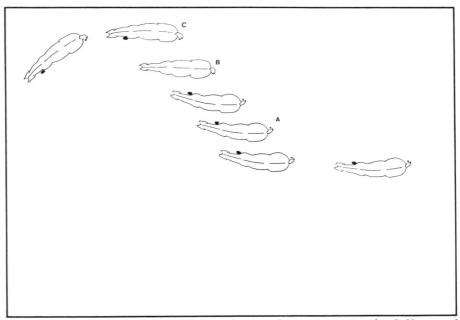

The preparation for the flying change. Ride down the center line in canter; A, ride a half pass to the wall; and B and C, ride a simple change.

horse thoroughly understands the canter depart, it will not be difficult to do the flying change.

In preparation for the change, ride a half pass in canter from the center line to the wall and make a simple change of lead through the walk when the horse reaches the wall. Do this three or four times, then ask for another half pass in the same place and upon reaching the wall, ask for a flying change. Timing is of the essence in the change. The horse can easily change the pattern of its legs during the moment of suspension when all four feet are off the ground, so your aid should come at the same time as the leading leg swings forward, the moment before suspension. Change the position of your legs, and give the aid for the new canter depart. *A flying change is nothing but a canter depart in canter.* The horse can already depart from the trot, walk, rein back, and halt, so it should be able to make a canter depart from the opposite canter lead.

Be doubly careful to give accurate light aids. Don't try to throw the horse's forehand over to the new lead; this only makes it difficult for the horse to change as it is no longer in balance. You want the change to be straight and you want the canter to remain light and cadenced. Don't give so strong an aid that the horse rushes off.

Ask for only one or two changes for the first few lessons; let the horse accept the new idea gradually. Once you can get a change to the "easy" lead, you can then try for the other change in the same way. Do all the preparatory steps again;

just because the horse can change from right to left, for instance, does not mean it can change from left to right. It's a whole new idea.

When the horse can do changes on either lead, take your time to perfect the single change. It is best to keep the first changes down the side of the arena as the horse stays straighter. When close to the wall, begin by riding a simple change to counter-canter at the beginning of the long side, asking for the change immediately after the horse comes through the short end. Interestingly, race horses on the track go round the ends of the track in true canter and switch to counter-canter on the straightaway. Once the horse performs the simple change easily, ride the horse through the short end in canter, straighten it, and ask for a flying

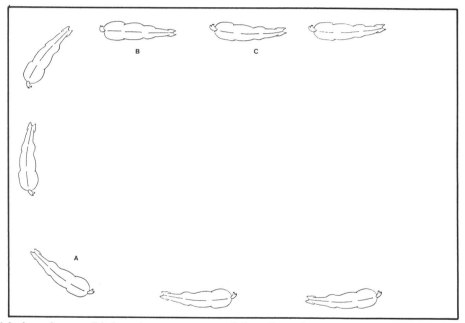

If the horse has a well balanced canter, you can ask for a flying change to counter canter at the beginning of the long side as you straighten after the corner: A, canter; B, straighten; and C, change.

change to counter-canter. This has the advantage of making the change very straight as the horse is held by the wall. When you can do single changes on the long side, you can then try for a single change on the diagonal. Beware of letting the horse become crooked.

When the single changes are solid, you can begin to ride changes in sequence. Ride a change at the beginning of the long side, one in the middle, and one at the end. Try for three changes every six strides on the diagonal. Reduce the number of strides in between until you can manage three changes every fourth stride. If the horse is speeding up, reduce your demands and return to the single changes. If you take time to perfect each stage, the sequential changes fall into your lap.

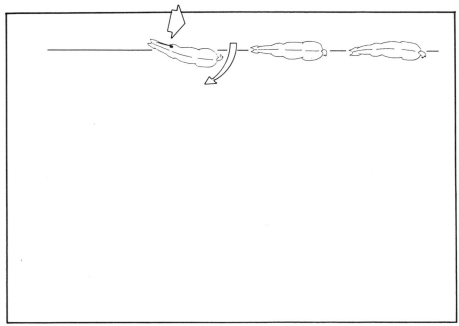

If you change the position of the head and neck too much to obtain the changes, the quarters will swing and the changes will be crooked.

If the horse begins to swing the hindquarters in the changes, be sure you are not changing the position of its head too much when you give the aids. You actually want to keep the horse's head and neck almost straight as you begin sequential changes because when you get to the changes every stride you cannot let the head swing from side to side; you will never have straight changes if you do. Also be careful that you are not taking your leg back too far, which can push the hindquarters out of line. Correct flying changes do not deviate from a straight line.

The changes every stride are a "trick," there is no real canter stride involved. The horse skips from one lead to the other, but the three beats of canter are absent: the horse skips from left hind and right fore to right hind and left fore.

To teach the changes every stride you must have the horse perfectly calm in the changes every fourth, third and second stride. By this time you will have a clear idea as to which change is easier for the horse. To teach the changes every stride, begin by putting the horse on the "easy" lead in counter-canter down the track. Ask the horse for a change to true canter, and as the horse begins to change reverse your aids and ask for the "easy" lead. Your aids must be quick and crystal clear, and your legs totally relaxed. Let the wall keep the horse straight and try

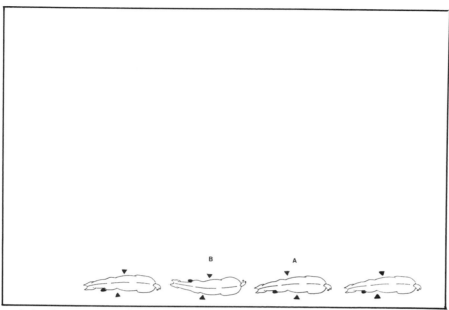

To teach the change every stride, begin by putting the horse on the "easy" lead in counter-canter. A, ask the horse for a change to true canter; and B, as the horse begins to change, reverse your aids. You must try to keep the horse as straight as possible, and just use your legs like a series of electric shocks with little or no rein aids to maintain the straightness.

not to do too much with the hands. The sequence is: as the leading leg swings forward, you ask for the change; as the horse swings the new leading leg forward, you ask for the original lead. Touch-touch. When the horse has given you two changes in succession, reward it and put it away for the day.

Continue your lessons in this way and be content with two changes. You can alternate the demand by asking from true canter to counter-canter to true canter. Take all the time you need to perfect these two changes on both leads. If the horse gets excited, stop the work for a week or so and go back to fours, threes, and single changes until the horse is quiet again. There is always a great temptation to do this work too quickly with the result the horse becomes excited and rushes; the result being your changes will never be confirmed. *Don't upset your horse in this work.* As we said before, there is more than one road to Rome and Rome was not built in a day!

When you can get two changes, try for four. Once you can get four calmly, you can increase the number. The important thing is that the horse remain both calm and straight. When you practice the changes every stride, always go back and ride the two-time changes at the end of the lesson to reestablish the canter strides.

The flying changes every stride.

The horse is finishing the left lead stride, with the leading leg supporting the weight so that,

the left leg can jump through and support the horse as it brings the right fore and hind leg forward.

The horse rotates over the right fore and brings the...

left hind and fore forward again.

Left lead,

back to the same moment as photo 1,

right lead,

leading leg in support,

and the new lead reaches through.

By this time the horse has fallen too much on the forehand after the repeated efforts, and it is harder for him to

lift up in front in order to change legs.

But the rider pushes him forward and refreshes the impulsion,

and he is able to jump through more successfully,

and take a balanced stride on the left lead.

⋄9⋄
COLLECTION, EXTENSION, AND IN BETWEEN

Collection, just what is it? All too often it is the missing ingredient in a dressage performance. To train and show successfully, you must have a crystal clear image in your mind as to the requirements for each exercise and understand the underlying principles of dressage.

The FEI definition of collection reads like a typical committee report; I'll try to translate in the italics:

1. **The aim of collection of the horse is:**

    1.1 **To further develop and improve the balance and equilibrium of the horse, which has been more or less displaced by the additional weight of the rider.**

    To rebalance the horse under the rider's weight.

    1.2 **To develop and increase the horse's ability to lower and engage his quarters for the benefit of the lightness and mobility of his forehand.**

    To activate and bend the hindquarters so they bear more weight and thus free up the forehand.

    1.3 **To add to the "ease and carriage" of the horse and make him more pleasurable to ride.**

    To rebalance and supple the horse making it easier to ride.

2. **The best means to obtain these aims are the lateral movements, travers, renvers, and last but not least, shoulder-in as well as half halts.**

Here the Rule Book is inconsistent, it lists the lateral work as leg-yielding, shoulder-in, travers, renvers and half pass in that order, but only includes travers, renvers and shoulder-in as lateral exercises for collection. The translation "last but not least" is a poor one as the original French word is "surtout"—above all.

So, the best means to obtain these aims are the lateral movements, travers, renvers, and above all shoulder-in as well as half pass and the use of half halts.

3. Collection is, in other words, improved and effected by engaging the hind legs, with the joints bent and supple, forward under the horse's body by a temporary but often repeated action of the seat and legs of the rider, driving the horse forward towards a more or less stationary or restraining hand, allowing just enough impulsion to pass through. Collection is consequently not achieved by shortening of the pace through a resisting action of the hand, but instead by using the seat and legs to engage the hind legs further under the horse's body.

Confused? The above wording is from the official FEI Rule Book and, as in many translations, an attempt to be literal has confused the issue. French is an exact language and often hard to translate word for word.

Collection is achieved by creating greater engagement of the hindlegs with increased bending and suppleness of the joints so they step up under the body of the horse. The seat and legs of the rider act to drive the horse up to the bridle in a series of light pushing actions. The hands receive the impulsion and regulate it. Collection is not the result of shortening the stride by use of the hands, but the result of using the seat and legs to engage the hind legs under the body.

4. However, the hind legs should not be engaged too far forward under the horse as this would shorten the base of support too much, and thereby impede the movement. In such a case, the line of the back would be lengthened and raised in relation to the supporting base of the legs, the stability would be deranged and the horse would have difficulty in finding a harmonious and correct balance.

I don't know about the stability being deranged, but my mind gets deranged trying to read this section! No wonder the idea of collection is misunderstood.

The hindlegs, however, must not step so far under the body that the base of support becomes too short. If the base is overshortened the spine will be stretched in opposition and the horse's balance will be compromised.

5. On the other hand, a horse with too long a base of support, unable or unwilling to engage his hind legs forward under the body, will never achieve an acceptable collection, characterized by "ease and carriage" as well as a lively impulsion originated in the activity of the quarters.

6. The position of the head and neck of a horse at the collected paces is naturally dependent on the stage of training and, in some degree, on his conformation. It should, however, be distinguished by the neck being raised unrestrained, forming a harmonious curve from the withers to the poll, being the highest point, with the head slightly in front of the vertical. However, at the moment the rider applies his aids in order to obtain a momentary and passing collecting effect, the head may become more or less vertical.

In collected paces the position of the head and neck will depend upon the stage of training of each horse and to an extent on individual conformation. The neck should be unrestrained and raised up in a curve to the poll which remains the highest point. The head should remain slightly in front of the vertical. However, when the rider applies a temporary half halt or collecting action of the seat the head can for an instant become almost vertical.

Collected trot, with joints bent and supple. Collection engages the hindquarters and lightens the forehand. Note the soft, supple contact on rein.

To sum up, collection is the result of increased engagement of the hindquarters and lively impulsion. The rider is collecting the forces of the horse and using those forces to produce active, supple, gymnastic movement.

The opposite side of the coin from collection is extension. True extension in all three gaits can not be developed until the horse can be collected.

The Rule Book is easier to understand in the description of extended paces.

403   4.3   Extended walk. The horse covers as much ground as possible without haste and without losing the regularity of his steps, the hind feet touching the ground clearly in front of the footprints of the fore feet. The rider allows the horse to stretch out his head and neck without, however, losing contact with the mouth.

Extended trot. The horse covers as much ground as possible.

Extended trot. This horse has exceptional action in front. This is good provided the hind legs engage as they do here. Some horses just flip their front legs.

Energetic, well rounded extended trot. Exceptionally nice.

COLLECTION, EXTENSION, AND IN BETWEEN

404 4.4 Extended trot. The horse covers as much ground as possible. Maintaining the same cadence he lengthens his steps to the utmost as a result of great impulsion from the hindquarters. The rider allows the horse, remaining "on the bit" without leaning on it, to lengthen his frame and to gain ground. The fore feet should touch the ground on the spot towards which they are pointing. The whole movement should be well balanced and the transition to collected trot should be smoothly executed by taking more weight on the hindquarters.

Here again the translation leaves a little to be desired. The French text states that the horse should lengthen the frame to avoid an exaggerated lifting of the forelegs, and that the front feet should not be drawn back as they touch the ground.

Extended canter. The horse covers as much ground as possible. Note the inside hind leg reaching up under the body.

405 4.4 Extended canter. The horse covers as much ground as possible. Maintaining the same rhythm, he lengthens his strides to the utmost, without losing any of his calmness and lightness, as a result of great impulsion from the hindquarters. The rider allows the horse, remaining "on the bit," without leaning on it, to lower and extend his head and neck, the tip of his nose pointing more or less forward.

The key words in all three descriptions are "The rider allows the horse to stretch out his head and neck—to lengthen his frame—to lower and extend his head and neck." If the horse is properly "on the bit" when the rider relaxes the arm muscles and stretches forward with the hand, it will automatically follow with the head and neck and lengthen its frame. You cannot lengthen successfully by restricting the neck.

To engage the hindquarters for medium or extended movements, the rider can take the legs slightly back in the beginning of the movement to drive the hindquarters up. Extensions and medium work should never given the appearance of running downhill.

Between collected and extended paces lie several steps. The Rule Book includes:

Free walk—a pace of relaxation in which the horse is allowed complete freedom to lower and stretch out his head and neck; and Medium walk— a free, regular and unconstrained walk of moderate extension. The horse, remaining 'on the bit,' walks energetically but calmly, with even and determined steps and the hindfeet touching the ground in front of the footprints of the fore feet. The rider maintains a light, soft and steady contact with the mouth.

The use of the word "free" in this definition is misleading. It is a translation of the French word "franc" better translated as "unconstrained."

No such gait as "free" trot exists, but the Rule Book notes a "working trot":

Working trot. Freely forward but lower and less engaged. Rider rises to allow horse to warm up easily.

This is a pace between the collected and medium trot in which a horse, not yet trained and ready for collected movements, shows himself properly balanced and remaining 'on the bit,' goes forward with even elastic steps and good hock action. The expression 'good hock action' does not mean that collection is a required quality of working trot; it only underlies the importance of an impulsion originated from the activity of the hindquarters.

The medium trot is a pace between the working and extended trot, but more 'round' than the latter. The horse goes forward with free and moderately extended steps and an obvious impulsion from the hind quarters. The rider allows the horse, remaining 'on the bit' to carry his head a little more in front of the vertical than at the collected trot and the working trot, and allows him at the same time to lower his head and neck slightly. The steps should be as even as possible, and the whole movement balanced and unconstrained.

The medium trot needs lots of "bounce per ounce," contains a good moment of suspension, but does not have the full thrust and ground-devouring stride of the extended trot.

Working canter and medium canter are also defined in the Rule Book:

Working canter—this is a pace between the collected and the medium canter, in which a horse, not yet trained and ready for collected movements, shows himself properly balanced and, remaining 'on the bit,' goes forward with even, light and cadenced strides and good hock action. The expression 'good hock action' does not mean that collection is a required quality of working canter. It only underlines the importance of an impulsion originated from the activity of the hindquarters.

Medium canter—this is a pace between the working and extended canter. The horse goes forward with free, balanced and moderately extended strides and on obvious impulsion from the hindquarters. The rider allows the horse, remaining 'on the bit' to carry his head a little more in front of the vertical than at the collected and working canter, and allows him at the same time to lower his head and neck slightly. The strides should be long and as even as possible, and the whole movement balanced and unconstrained.

In all the definitions, these facts stand out: the horse must remain balanced and unconstrained. Nowhere is there any mention of a change of speed, even in the working gaits. The horse must be in balance and able to stay "in the hand." The term "on the bit" is not an exact translation of the French. The original French term is "dans la main," or "in the hand."

The Half Halt

"They seek him here
They seek him there
Those Frenchies seek him everywhere
Is he in heaven
Or is he in hell
That demmed elusive ~~Pimpernel~~ Half Halt."

As this chapter started by wondering just what collection is, perhaps we should consider the nature of the half halt, without which we cannot obtain collection. Back to the Rule Book:

The half halt is a hardly visible, almost simultaneous co-ordinated action of the seat, the legs and the hand of the rider, with the object of increasing the attention and balance of the horse before the execution of several movements or transitions to lesser and higher paces. In shifting slightly more weight onto the horse's quarters, the engagement of the hind legs and the balance on the haunches are facilitated, for the benefit of the forehand and the horse's balance as a whole.

Well and good, "but just what is a half-halt?" you are probably still wondering.

As the horse moves forward in any given gait, the rider needs to prepare it for a transition from one gait to another, or within the same gait, or to rebalance the horse, so it can start a new exercise. That's when you execute a half halt. You lift your upper body, stretch your spine, press both your legs against the horse's sides, and close your hands on the reins—seat-leg-hand. In effect you are driving the horse into your hands, which catch the surge of energy. As soon as you have applied these aids, you relax them—the secret of giving a half halt is to stop as soon as you have applied the pressure. The horse, in response to your driving and retarding aid, draws itself together in preparation for a transition but finds that you are now asking it to go forward again. It's like gearing down a racing car for a turn: you gear down and accelerate through the turn, at least you do if you want to make speed. You rock the horse back towards its quarters, then ask it to use that added impetus. In later training the horse will often be attentive enough that merely lifting your upper body will give you the effect you desire. In the beginning stages you can develop the half halt through the complete halt. Trot—halt, trot—halt, trot—start to halt—but trot on instead.

Many riders make the mistake of waiting too long to feel the effect of the half halt, by which time it has lost the effectiveness. *Don't wait for it, give the correct aids and ride on*; trust your horse to react. You do not want to squash the impulsion but to augment it through increased thrust from engaged quarters. A half halt is not just an action of the rein; it is a coordinated sequence of actions from seat, legs and hands given in a brief second. If the horse ignores the aids, it is better to repeat the action than to hold and wait for the result. If you wait and hold, the horse will lose all impulsion and dive on the rein.

◇ 10 ◇
PIAFFE

When do you begin to teach a horse to execute a piaffe? When it is ready. And how do you know when it is ready? With some horses you can teach the piaffe quite early as it is an excellent exercise for the hindquarters. But, in general, horses can begin to learn the piaffe when they are capable of a collected trot and have been in muscle-building training for nine months or so.

Piaffe and passage are the ultimate exercises in the education of the horse, and training a horse to these gymnastics takes some experience. If the rider has never ridden a horse trained in these exercises, it is well nigh impossible to go about teaching them. Take the time to find a school with trained horses. Barring that, find an experienced rider who is willing to give you the "feel" on horses that already know the exercises. Mistakes made in training the piaffe or passage will result in confused, tense horses.

How do you decide whether to teach the piaffe first or the passage first? That depends upon the individual horse, its conformation, natural ability and temperament. For the horse with superb balance and a natural suspension in trot, passage comes easily. For the average horse, or the horse with a long back and poor balance, the piaffe can help to make the horse round and balanced.

If the horse is accustomed to the work in hand, teaching the piaffe comes as a natural progression of the other exercises. I find that if the piaffe is started from the ground, the horse can grasp the requirements in a short period of work. The horse is already used to the rider on the ground and the use of the whip to activate the hindquarters, and can accept the new demands.

However, at first the horse may have difficulty in understanding the concept of lifting its feet while remaining on the spot. Once that idea is established in its mind, the rest comes with practice.

For the first lessons I usually put the lungeing cavesson back on over the bridle so that I have control over the horse's head without having to resort to the use of the reins. I attach a short lead shank to the ring of the cavesson so I don't have to hold an entire lunge line rolled up in my hand.

I place the horse facing left against the wall at the beginning of the long side.

You don't want to start the exercise going into a corner or on the short end; instead, start coming out of a corner. I take the left rein by the bit, and hold the lead rope in my left hand. The right hand holds a long swishy whip as well as the right rein across the neck by the wither. The right rein is important to keep the horse straight.

Tap the horse on top of the quarters with the whip. The piaffe has to be performed with well bent hindquarters, and the idea of lowering the quarters must be introduced at the very beginning. If you tap the horse's hindlegs, it will merely pick up its feet and not perform the piaffe through a swinging, supple back. As you use the whip, the horse will probably take a step forward; let it advance just a little but not too much. Then halt it and try again; as the horse moves forward, use the reins to contain it. The horse will probably get somewhat excited. You ask it to move, then you stop it—it cannot understand this new demand. Gently rein it back a couple of steps to place it back onto its quarters and tap again. If the horse gives you even the slightest lifting of the hind feet with a bouncy feeling, stop, praise it, and feed it a goodie. You need a good supply of treats before you even begin this lesson, so fill your pockets with sugar or your horse's treat of choice.

Some horses get frustrated and excited in the beginning and will plunge forward right through your hand. If this happens, you may well need an assistant on the lead rope to prevent the horse from walking right through you. Sharp snatches on the cavesson will bring the horse back into position. You have to persevere in the first week or two. Once the horse has caught on, the training becomes just a matter of time but the initial stages can take many days. You have to be quick to reward even an indication of understanding. The horse may just lift up the hind legs at the beginning and that is good. You then have to work

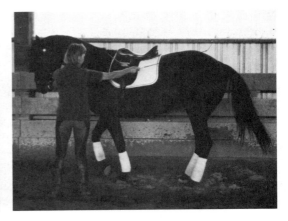

Evolution of piaffe.
1. Tap the horse on the croup until he picks up a hind leg.

2. Sometimes the horse just moves the front feet but plants the hind feet. Horse has tipped onto front end.

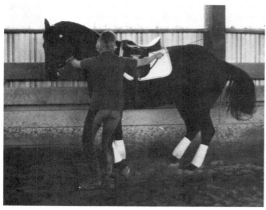

3. *Advance with the horse, taking small steps yourself. Here the horse begins to bend the joints and come under, raising the forehand.*

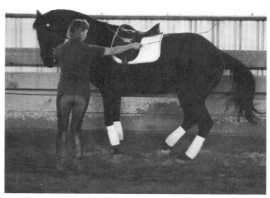

4. *The joints are bending and the horse is almost springing from one leg to the other.*

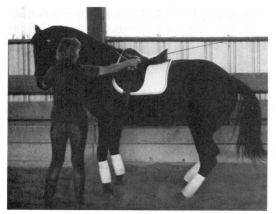

5. *He comes more and more under and elevates the forehand as a direct result of bending the quarters.*

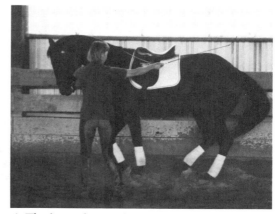

6. *The first real steps of active piaffe.*

on getting it to lift a diagonal pair of legs; otherwise, the horse just steps from one leg to the other. Let the horse creep forward as it lifts its legs and the diagonals will begin to work together; you can remain on the spot later on.

Eventually the horse will grasp the concept and then it is up to you to work a few moments in piaffe daily until the horse can spring from diagonal to diagonal for three or four steps without getting upset. Be content with very few steps at the beginning and the horse will be able to piaffe for a long time afterwards. Better to have four good rhythmic steps than fourteen rushed and tense leg liftings.

One of the dangers of touching one hind leg with the whip is that the horse will depend upon the whip as an aid and will lift the leg nearest the trainer higher than the one furthest away, developing an uneven stepping or snatching one hind leg up while the other remains on the ground. If the horse "sits" down from the croup, it will lift both legs evenly and will use its spine and body in a vibrant, even piaffe.

The piaffe, mounted. At the beginning, have someone assist from the ground as the horse will already understand the concept.

The rider sits quietly and stretches up with a light contact. The horse sits easily and springs from leg to leg. This is quite sufficient for the beginning stages; later on, you can afford to ask for more height and spring. But at these early stages, rhythm and relaxation are the most important elements so the horse does not become excited.

Piaffe can also be taught from the saddle by riders who have had much experience. When the trot becomes well collected and the horse balanced, you can use trot to rein back and trotting forward again to introduce the idea. You gradually ask for less and less backward motion and perform half steps forward. The trick here is to maintain the diagonal stepping of the legs in the rhythm of trot until the horse is almost on the spot, but still in a trot rhythm. *Again one or two steps is sufficient in the beginning.* Don't lose the rhythm or forward feeling at any point. Ask often and reward the moment you get any appreciable result. Once you get the glimmering of understanding, let the horse know and stop for that day. Many short sessions in teaching piaffe are better than spending hours at it, ending up with horse and rider frustrated and exhausted. Work on vigorous forward movements in between lessons in piaffe.

In the Grand Prix test, 10 to 12 steps of piaffe are required; that's not that many. I once had the opportunity of watching Nuno Oliveira schooling a talented young stallion who was gifted far beyond the average in the piaffe. He put the horse into a piaffe at X going across the center of the school. I was chatting to another student beside me in the gallery and happened to glance at my watch.

The "goodie" jar is a necessary part of training—reward often!

The piaffe continued, the horse lifting diagonal pairs of legs and champing softly on the bridle with the reins stretched and relaxed. I glanced again at my watch *15 minutes later*: the piaffe was still in place. The horse was still relaxed, still stepping even higher than before. I shall never forget that moment; it represents the ultimate in mastery of the piaffe. At the end, the horse was certainly wet with exertion, but his mind remained calm throughout.

Not many horses will be able to piaffe for 15 minutes, but most horses can manage some type of piaffe. Those with weak backs will never achieve a spectacular movement, but even the weak horse can show even and balanced steps that emanate from bent and engaged hindquarters and a supple, relaxed body.

The aids for the piaffe are individual to each horse. Generally, the rider must move the lower leg further back than for any other exercise to ensure good bending of the hindquarters. I try to find a place on the horse's sides that I do not use for any other movement except the piaffe. The rider's back and leg must remain completely without contraction so that the horse can utilize its spine to the utmost. The first time you sit on a horse in piaffe, you can feel the muscles of the horse's back vibrating and pulsing under the saddle and can appreciate just how important they are to the horse's ability to perform.

The rider's back and upper body must remain stretched and totally relaxed to allow the horse the use of its back and entire body in the piaffe. The rider's legs must stay soft, with the heel and spur in contact with the horse's sides. In the beginning you can use your voice to good effect, especially if you have employed it when teaching the horse from the ground. The whip can be used gently on the horse's croup to reinforce the heels. You are aiming for a soft swinging exercise, and should end by letting the horse come to a halt, loosening the reins, and letting the horse relax forward in a calm walk. You do not want to go energetically forward into piaffe in the early stages, but to allow the horse to relax totally so it comes to enjoy the demands of the piaffe and not to resent them.

◊ 11 ◊

PASSAGE

Passage is the *ne plus ultra* form of the collected trot. All horses are capable of passage but not all horses will produce the same passage. Some will show high action, some a more rounded action, while others show a short lively action. Whatever form, the passage must remain even and forward in feeling, without any side to side swing. The quarters should be well engaged and the forehand well elevated. The characteristic of passage is the height of the steps and the increased suspension of the entire mass. The horse springs from one diagonal pair of legs to the other; passage appears to be in slow motion with the horse's back developing a tremendous amount of swing.

Passage is natural to the horse. Horses in the field will elevate their heads and necks and bounce from one diagonal to the other if startled or excited. The latent ability to do the movement is there; your job is to produce it upon request. You don't want to have to overexcite your horse to achieve passage; you must find another method.

The horses used as models for the old engravings of the High School passage were usually related to the andalusian, iberian, or "Spanish" horses. They had powerful quarters, high knee action and produced a highly elevated passage. The thoroughbred type of horse was developed to have longer lower strides to cover the ground in racing, and will show a lower, longer stride in the passage. The action of the passage will also vary according to the build of the horse. Given this premise, it is incorrect to state that the legs must be raised to such and such a point for the passage; it will vary greatly.

To teach the passage, the rider needs to show the horse how to prolong the suspension of the diagonal, and it is easier to tackle one diagonal at a time. If you try to achieve passage directly from the collected trot, the horse will not necessarily understand the difference. The beats in trot are too close together; the rider would have to alternate aids so rapidly the horse would not have time to understand and would probably become agitated and confused.

The main difficulty in passage is convincing the horse that it must jump from one diagonal to the other, and not just trot. Here, the use of the half halt really

Passage.

comes into play. You begin by asking the horse for trot—halt—trot transitions, making sure that it moves forward promptly. Then, collect the trot with long half halts, almost halting the horse by prolonging the aid, and then asking the horse immediately to move forward again. With luck, the horse will begin to spring more energetically forward. You can use medium trot in between asking for passage so the horse retains the impulsion.

The rhythm of the passage is slow and regular, and the horse must understand the need to spring from one set of legs to the other. A frequent problem is losing impulsion when you use the half halts; there must be a careful balance between the retarding and driving aid.

With horses that work well in hand, you can get good results when mounted by using the whip on top of the croup to make the horse engage and jump forward at the same time, giving you more power. Each horse is different; you will find the best way to communicate by trying several approaches to see which the horse understands best.

Sometimes it is easier for the horse to understand one set of commands at a time. When he has grasped the concept, then you can merge the alternate diagonals. However, once the horse has understood the demand, the rider must then put the exercise into its proper form.

The first lesson in passage should come at the end of a training session when the horse is in good balance, attentive, on the aids, and full of impulsion. Ride the horse on a 10-meter circle to the left. The correctly ridden circle requires the horse to take a slightly longer stride with the right fore than the left, and engages the left hind more than the right. This means the right diagonal is already making more effort. The rider brings the horse's shoulders slightly to the inside as if asking for left shoulder-in, while the right rein should be brought to bear on the neck to bring the weight of the forehand inside. The rider's left leg remains at the girth to keep the bend and to encourage the left hind to retain the engagement, while the right leg remains slightly back to prevent the right hindleg from drifting out of the circle.

Using a half halt with the right rein against the neck as the left fore comes into support and using the left leg at the same time, try to prolong the moment of support of the left diagonal and the suspension of the right diagonal. You can use a touch of the whip on the right shoulder as the left fore swings forward and down. It will take some time before the horse offers a higher gesture with the right front and any indication of this must be immediately rewarded. It may take several days for the horse to understand what you want. Once you can get one or two clearly marked liftings of the right foreleg, reverse the circle and try the same tactics to the right. The horse needs to take a definite spring into the air with the outside foreleg.

After you get the horse to give you one or two steps on either side, you must then try to "marry" the two gestures as soon as possible. Otherwise you will only succeed in encouraging the horse to favor its weaker side.

Once you can get the gesture on the circle, try to obtain one or two steps on the straightaway near the wall. The hands will act alternately on the leg that is on the ground, while the legs are also used alternately on the opposite hind leg.

Some horses will give the required lift easily on one diagonal, but have trouble on the other. Work patiently and carefully, and never scold the horse for offering more than you ask at the beginning. Horses with good natural suspension in the trot may well offer you several steps in succession fairly early in the lesson. Reward them and walk. For the nervous horse, be content with one or two steps at a time until the horse accepts the demands. At no time should you be concerned about the height of the steps in the early lessons; it is only important that the horse learns to prolong the steps. Height can come later when the horse has mastered the cadence of the exercise.

When the horse understands the passage and can manage several elevated steps, you can increase the demands.

The final task is to move from passage to piaffe and on to passage again. This transition is the stumbling block for many horses. The horse that has learned the passage first often has trouble in reducing the passage to the piaffe, while the horse that has learned the piaffe first often has trouble in moving forward in a proper passage. The move requires the utmost tact and sensitivity on the part of the rider.

The work on passage and piaffe takes place over several months, not necessarily beginning at the same time, but once you begin to teach the second exercise, you must think about "marrying" the two. For the horse that has begun to passage first, gradually reduce the forward steps until the passage barely creeps forward.

Let the horse "dwell" for two or three steps, then let it jump forward again. You are letting the horse passage "in place" as it were. Your upper body and spine indicate the amount of forward movement you want, while the legs remain close and slide further back as you reduce the passage. As you want the horse to swing forward again, you make a definite change in the use of your legs. In passage the legs give alternate squeezes, while the hands give and take in opposition. In piaffe the hands serve to hold the reins so the horse remains straight and as relaxed as possible, giving little checks if the horse moves forward, while the legs remain quiet and the heels closed. The horse must be in true self carriage for the piaffe.

The horse that has learned piaffe first will have more trouble in moving forward into passage. What you get at the beginning is a "creeping" piaffe with low steps; you must encourage the thrust of the hindleg and ask the horse to spring forward with greater ground-gaining strides.

This transition from passage to piaffe and to passage again takes a long time to perfect. In the beginning be content with reduced variations of both airs. Again, the height of the steps is less important at this stage than the smoothness with which the horse passes from one exercise to the other. Allot the space of an *entire year's work* before you think about showing this transition in public.

A horse that has truly superior suspension in the collected trot can be asked to passage by moving between a forward collection to a reduced collection with emphasis on the alternative use of your leg aids, a retarding action of the opposing hand, and an increased swinging action of your back. Not many horses are suitable for this method.

As another alternative you can use cavaletti to encourage and introduce the passage, *only if cavaletti have been included in the basic training of your horse.* Don't rush out and buy cavaletti just to teach the passage. The horse that has been worked over groundpoles in the early stages, as all young horses should be as far as I am concerned, no matter what their future, will not be upset by a new pattern of poles. Set the cavaletti at the second height, 14 inches at three and a half to four feet apart, depending upon the length of the horse's natural stride. Do not use more than four cavaletti for this work. Approach the gymnastic in collected trot and let the horse "bounce" through. One great advantage in using cavaletti is that you ensure the even activity of the horse's hind legs: it has to spring upwards to clear the poles. As the horse reaches the last pole, try to maintain the same bounce for a few more strides. This method is useful for the horse that is tight in its shoulders because it has to raise its forefeet to avoid knocking the poles.

I am sure many "purists" will disagree with this technique to which I can only say, "If it is good enough for Reiner Klimke, it's good enough for me." Klimke outlines the work in his excellent little book entitled *Cavaletti.*

EPILOGUE

The fruit of your training program should be a horse that is developed to the full extent of its natural talent. The road to that goal is long and frustrating, but the rewards are great.

Along the way you will want to show your horse in competitions to gauge your training methods and for the sake of competing against others. The horse could care less about competition, and could probably care less about working also. So we should always bear in mind that it is *our* satisfaction to show; the horse, because of its willingness, goes along with us. Athletic competition in other disciplines involves only the human athlete. It is our decision to push ourselves to the point of exhaustion for our own personal satisfaction, but when it comes to equestrian sport we should always bear in mind that the horse is part of the endeavor, and should never be abused in the name of competition.

Show your horse off by all means, but don't make competition the end goal. Make the training of the horse to realize its potential your goal. We have a responsibility to the horse—competition and its attendant pressures should be kept in perspective.

Competition should be included in the training program as a barometer of progress. If your score sheets reflect scores of 60 percent and better, with few marks of 5 or below, you are on the right track. If you score consistently in the 50's or below, something is wrong with your program.

Dressage tests are progressive and indicate the training program. They are not just a bunch of movements thrown together by a committee (although I must admit sometimes I have my doubts about some tests!). The difficulty of the exercises and the expectations increase up through the national levels to the international FEI tests. Training and First Level are the beginning stages for the horse in its first six months of training. Second and Third Level establish a spring board for advanced training. Any horse, no matter what its role in life, can benefit from Training up to Third Level; this is too often neglected nowadays. This basic work used to be known as the Campaign School and was included in the education of all horses. Fourth Level leads to Prix St. Georges and is within reach of most horses. From then on, the requirements are more specialized and designed to test the gifted horses who will continue on to the High School.

The separation comes when true collection is needed; without collection the advanced movements are unattainable. Horses can be taught the "tricks" but without collection, there is no real dressage.

Dressage after all means training, and training develops the horse's natural ability and mind. The fully trained horse should be an athlete performing willing and brilliantly the complicated movements based on natural skills, but refined to the highest level. If this is so, dressage is indeed an art. If the horse is used for the purpose of the rider's ego in winning competition points dressage is no longer an art but an abuse of a generous long-suffering animal.

INDEX